A Guide to the Lectionary

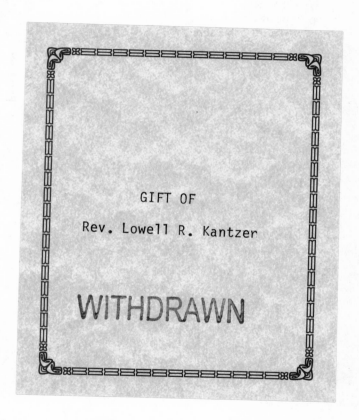

A Guide to the
LECTIONARY

Ann Brooke Bushong

A Crossroad Book

THE SEABURY PRESS · NEW YORK

124711

1978 · *The Seabury Press*
815 Second Avenue · New York, N.Y. 10017

Printed in the United States of America
Library of Congress Cataloging in Publication Data

Bushong, Ann Brooke,   A guide to the lectionary.
"A Crossroad book."
"A new and completely revised edition."
1. Lectionaries.   2. Bible—Liturgical lessons, English.   I. Protestant Episcopal Church in the U. S. A. Liturgical Commission. The draft proposed Book of common prayer. The lectionary. II. Title.
BX5947.L4B84   1978   264′.032   77-17046   ISBN 0-8164-2156-0

In memoriam

The Rev. Walter B. McKinley
and Kitty Stigers McKinley,
my grandparents;
Kitty Blair Frank, my godmother;
and E. Stuart Bushong,
my father.

Requiescant in pace

Contents

Preface

This Guide to the Lectionary is a new and completely revised edition in one volume of the three volumes formerly distributed by the Church Army in the U.S.A. It incorporates all the features of previous editions, as well as some new ones.

Originally, this Guide was developed for a narrow purpose. I was working with the Church School at the Church of St. Mary the Virgin in New York City when the Rector, the Rev. Donald L. Garfield, wondered out loud whether the new lectionary scheme could be developed into a three-year Church School curriculum. I began to explore the implications of this question, and, by way of preparation, worked out many of the connections between the various Sunday readings. I then checked my work with Capt. Howard E. Galley, Jr., of the Church Army, and, in addition to helping me with the interrelationships between the readings for each Sunday, he pointed out that there were possibilities for wider applicability and use in the Church. As a means of testing this thesis, we went to General Convention in 1970 with 300 mimeographed copies of Year C in hand, and were overwhelmed at the enthusiastic response. As a result, more copies were printed, and arrangements made for their distribution by the Church Army. Subsequently the Guide for Years A and B were published.

Thus, a guide which started as an exploration of the lectionary for use in a Church School curriculum has developed into a book which has proven to be of assistance to a much wider audience. Church musicians and clergy have written to tell us of its usefulness in planning Sunday services, and a number of people have used it as a guide in their personal meditations.

This new edition of the Guide incorporates the readings for the Sundays of all three years, together with those appointed for the major Holy Days.

My special thanks goes to my editor at the Seabury Press, Howard Galley, without whose encouragement and assistance over the past seven years this book would not have been possible.

Many persons have assisted in the preparation of the manuscript, and my thanks and appreciation goes to all of them: Sally Elliott, who prepared the workbooks which were so necessary to the job; Mason Martens, who prepared the Hymn Lists; Robert D. Gillespie, C.A., who assisted with the editing; the people at St. Clement's Church in New York City for their moral support, and especially Margaret Stall, who assisted with the proofreading.

Michaelmas 1977   A.B.B.

Introduction

This Guide to the Lectionary presents in table form a synopsis of each of the lessons and Psalms appointed for the Sundays of all three years of the lectionary cycle, as well as those appointed for the major Holy Days, as set forth in the Proposed Book of Common Prayer. The theme for the day, when there is one, appears in parentheses in the lefthand column. At least one Hymn is suggested for use on each Sunday and Holy Day. In addition, a suggested Alleluia Verse is provided for use before the Gospel, except in Lent when a Tract or Verse is provided instead.

Concerning the Lessons

In the Lectionary, the appointed readings are arranged in a three-year cycle: Year A being the Year of Matthew, Year B the Year of Mark, and Year C the Year of Luke. The plan is particularly evident on the "green Sundays" after Epiphany and after Pentecost when the Gospel of the Year is read semi-continuously from week to week. During the seasons of Advent, Christmas, Lent, and Easter, however, the lessons are chosen to illustrate traditional themes—frequent use being made (in all three years) of the Gospel according to John.

Usually, only two of the three lessons appointed for a Sunday tie together thematically. Most commonly, it is the Old Testament Lesson and the Gospel that are chosen to match, or to complement each other. Occasionally the Old Testament Lesson is chosen to match the Epistle. On special occasions, particularly when there is a traditional theme (such as on Christmas Day, Palm Sunday, Maundy Thursday, or Easter Day), all three lessons may pick up the theme of the occasion, without being directly connected with each other.

The Lessons appointed for use in this Lectionary are intended to be used at all public services on the particular Sunday or Holy Day for which they are appointed (except when the same congregation attends two or more services). The appointed lessons, therefore, should be used at the principal service of the day, whether the Liturgy of the Word takes the form given in the Holy Eucharist, or that of the Daily Office. (The Prayer Book, pages 47 and 84, makes specific provision for three readings at the Office.) If only two of the readings are used at the Office, it will frequently be found desirable to include the suggested lengthenings of the assigned lessons shown by parentheses.

On some occasions the lessons are the same in all three years. We have indicated such days by the note *ABC* in the lefthand column. When a theme is indicated, it usually stays the same in all three years even though the lessons may vary.

Information about the general plan and underlying principles of this Lectionary is given at various points throughout the Guide. (See also page 888 of the Prayer Book.)

Concerning the Psalms

The singing of a Psalm between the lessons is one of the most ancient (and interesting) features of the Church's eucharistic liturgy. The restoration of this has been made explicit by the assignment of a Psalm to each proper. In this Guide, we have provided two citations for each Psalm (traditionally called the Gradual Psalm), and by its order in the table suggested that it be sung or recited between the Old Testament Lesson and the Epistle. The first citation of the Psalm is taken from the Lectionary (pages 889–995). Whenever the Lectionary has provided a shorter version of the appointed Psalm, we have cited that version. Alternatively, we have provided a version of the Psalm arranged for responsorial use between a cantor and the congregation, and have included the text of a suggested refrain. Ordinarily, the refrain is drawn from, or adapted from, the Psalm appointed. When it is not, the source is cited in brackets. The normal method of performance is as follows:

Cantor sings Refrain
Choir and Congregation repeat Refrain
Cantor sings first group of verses
Choir and Congregation repeat Refrain
Cantor sings second set of verses
Choir and Congregation repeat Refrain, etc.

Traditionally, Gloria Patri is not added to Gradual Psalms. It is recommended that the congregation remain seated for the Psalm as it has a meditative quality which usually reflects back to the preceding lesson. Because of this connection, it is appropriate for the cantor to sing the Psalm from the lectern at which the lessons are read. Throughout the Easter season, "Hallelujah" is appointed as an alternative Refrain. A double or triple "Hallelujah" is intended.

Concerning the Alleluia Verses

The Alleluia verse, although not of as great antiquity or importance as the Gradual, can serve as a fitting expression of praise prior to the announcement of the Gospel. The usual method of performance is as follows:

Cantor sings Alleluia (one or more times)
Choir and Congregation repeat the Alleluia
Cantor sings Verse
Choir and Congregation repeat the Alleluia

When there is a Gospel procession, the Alleluia should not be begun until the procession has formed and is beginning to move. All stand.

Alternatives in Lent

In Lent, in place of the Alleluia, we have provided two alternative chants. The first is a Verse, based on modern Roman Catholic usage, and adapted to the Episcopal Lectionary. The second alternative is based on an older custom, and provides a second Psalm to be sung at this point. The Verse is sung by a cantor or by the choir. The Psalm (called a tract) is sung without refrain by a cantor, or by the choir, or alternatively (e.g., between men's and women's voices).

The Place of the Chants in the Service

When only the Gradual Psalm is used, it is sung after the First Reading. A Hymn ("Sequence") may be used after the Second Reading. When both the Gradual and Alleluia chants are used, the service is arranged in the following manner:

1. *When three Readings are used*
   Lesson
   Gradual Psalm
   Epistle*
   Alleluia (in Lent Tract or Verse)
   Gospel

2. *When two Readings are used*
   A.   Sundays and Holy Days
   Lesson or Epistle
   Gradual Psalm
   Alleluia (omitted in Lent)
   Gospel

   B.   Weekdays
   Lesson or Epistle
   Gradual Psalm *or* Alleluia
   Gospel

   * If a Sequence Hymn is also desired, it follows the Epistle and precedes the Alleluia.

Concerning the Hymns

A "Hymn of the Day" has been provided for each proper. Selected with reference to the Bible readings, it is recommended for use in close connection with them: before the Gospel, or after the Sermon, or during the Offertory.

Hymns in the list on pages 202–205 are arranged by seasons and by the appropriate place in the service. They are not assigned to specific Sundays.

The number of hymns has been kept within the limits of what average congregations may be expected to master.

Many familiar hymns have been included. A number of less familiar hymns has also been listed, some of which appear in the table more than once.

The hymns listed under "Dismissal" may be used before or after the postcommunion prayer when desired (see Prayer Book, page 409).

A Guide to the Lectionary

Year A

The Themes of the Advent Sundays are the same in all three years.

SEE PAGES 202–205 FOR OTHER SUGGESTED HYMNS	FIRST LESSON	PSALM
Year A 1 Advent (The final Advent) Hymn 440	Isaiah 2:1–5 Out of Zion shall go forth the law, and the word of the Lord from Jerusalem. He shall judge between the nations, and shall decide for many peoples.	Psalm 122 *or* **Refrain:** I was glad when they said to me, Let us go to the house of the Lord. *Psalm 122* 2,3,4/5,6,7/8,9
Year A 2 Advent (The Ministry of John the Baptist) Hymn 10	Isaiah 11:1–10 In that day the root of Jesse shall stand as an ensign to the peoples; him shall the nations seek.	Psalm 72:1–8 *or* **Refrain:** In his time, justice and peace shall flourish. *Psalm 72* 1, 2/3,4/5,6/7,8
Year A 3 Advent (The Ministry of John the Baptist) Hymn 2	Isaiah 35:1–10 The eyes of the blind shall be opened, and the ears of the deaf unstopped; then shall the lame man leap like a hart, and the tongue of the dumb (mute) man sing for joy.	Psalm 146:4–9 *or* **Refrain** (Isa. 35:4): Come, O Lord, and save us. *Psalm 146* 4,5/6,7/8,9

SECOND LESSON	CHANT BEFORE GOSPEL	GOSPEL
Romans 13:8–14	**Alleluia**	**Matthew 24:37–44**
Salvation is nearer to us now than when we first believed. Let us then cast off the works of darkness and put on the armor of light.	(Psalm 85:7) Show us your mercy, O Lord, * and grant us your salvation.	As were the days of Noah, so will be the coming of the Son of man. Two men will be in the field; one is taken and one is left. Be ready: for the Son of man is coming at an hour you do not expect.
Romans 15:4–13	**Alleluia**	**Matthew 3:1–12**
Christ became a servant to the circumcised to show God's truthfulness, in order to confirm the promises given to the patriarchs, and in order that the Gentiles might glorify God for his mercy.	(Luke 3:4,6) Prepare the way of the Lord, make his paths straight;* and all flesh shall see the salvation of our God.	John said (to the Pharisees and Sadducees), Bear fruit that befits repentance and do not presume to say . . . We have Abraham as our father . . . God is able from these stones to raise up children to Abraham.
James 5:7–10	**Alleluia**	**Matthew 11:2–11**
Be patient, therefore, brethren, until the coming of the Lord. As an example of suffering and patience . . . take the prophets.	(Luke 4:18) The Spirit of the Lord is upon me;* he has anointed me to preach good tidings to the poor.	John heard in prison about the deeds of the Christ . . . Are you he who is to come, or shall we look for another? Jesus answered, The blind receive their sight and the lame walk.

	FIRST LESSON	PSALM
Year A 4 Advent (The Annunciation) Hymn 317(1&2) or 329	**Isaiah 7:10–17** The Lord himself will give you a sign. Behold, a young woman shall conceive and bear a son.	**Psalm 24:1–7** *or* **Refrain:** Lift up your heads, O gates; and the King of glory shall come in. *Psalm 24* 1,2/3,4/5,6
Year ABC Christmas Day I (At Midnight) Hymn 20 or 42	**Isaiah 9:2–4, 6–7** The people who walked in darkness have seen a great light. For to us a child is born . . . and the government will be upon his shoulder.	**Psalm 96:1–4,11–12** *or* **Refrain** (Luke 2:11): Today is born our Savior, Christ the Lord. *Psalm 96* 1,2/3,4/11,12
Year ABC Christmas Day II (At Dawn) Hymn 13	**Isaiah 62:6–7,10–12** Say to the daughter of Zion, Behold, your salvation comes. They shall be called The holy people, The redeemed of the Lord.	**Psalm 97:1–4,11–12** *or* **Refrain** (Isa. 9:6): To us a child is born; to us a Son is given. *Psalm 97* 1,2/3,4/11,12
Year ABC Christmas Day III (During the Day) Hymn 18	**Isaiah 52:7–10** How beautiful upon the mountains are the feet of him who brings good tidings. All the ends of the earth shall see the salvation of our God.	**Psalm 98:1–6** *or* **Refrain:** All the ends of the earth have seen the salvation of our God. *Psalm 98* 1,2/3,4/5,6

[4]

SECOND LESSON	CHANT BEFORE GOSPEL	GOSPEL
Romans 1:1–7	**Alleluia**	**Matthew 1:18–25**
The Gospel of God which he promised beforehand through his prophets in the holy scriptures, the gospel concerning his Son, who was descended from David according to the flesh.	(Matt. 1:23) A virgin shall conceive and bear a son,* and his name shall be called Emmanuel.	An angel of the Lord appeared to him in a dream, saying, Joseph, son of David, do not fear to take Mary your wife, for that which is conceived in her is of the Holy Spirit. She will bear a son.
Titus 2:11–14	**Alleluia**	**Luke 2:1–14(15–20)**
The grace of God has appeared for the salvation of all . . . the appearing of the glory of our great God and Savior Jesus Christ.	(Luke 2:10,11) Behold, I bring you good tidings of great joy;* to you is born a Savior, Christ the Lord.	To you is born this day in the city of David a Savior, who is Christ the Lord.
Titus 3:4–7	**Alleluia**	**Luke 2:(1–14)15–20**
He saved us . . . by the washing of regeneration and renewal in the Holy Spirit.	(Luke 2:14) Glory to God in the highest,* and peace to his people on earth.	Let us go over to Bethlehem and see this thing that has happened, which the Lord has made known to us.
Hebrews 1:1–12	**Alleluia**	**John 1:1–14**
God spoke of old . . . by the prophets; but in these last days he has spoken to us by a Son . . . through whom also he created the world. Thou art my Son, today I have begotten thee.	(John 1:14) The Word was made flesh and dwelt among us,* full of grace and truth.	The Word became flesh and dwelt among us, full of grace and truth.

	FIRST LESSON	PSALM
Year ABC First Sunday after Christmas (The Incarnation) Hymn 17	Isaiah 61:10—62:3 The Lord God will cause righteousness and praise to spring forth before all the nations.	Psalm 147:13–21 *or* **Refrain** (John 1:14): The Word was made flesh and dwelt among us. *Psalm 147* 13,14/15,16/20,21
Year ABC The Holy Name of our Lord Jesus Christ January 1 Hymn 326	Exodus 34:1–8 Moses cut two tables of stone . . . and went up on Mount Sinai. The Lord descended in the cloud and stood with him there and proclaimed the name of the Lord.	Psalm 8 *or* **Refrain:** O Lord our Governor, how exalted is your Name in all the world. *Psalm 8* 4,5/6,7/8,9
Year ABC Second Sunday after Christmas (The Holy Family) Hymn 504 or 35	Jeremiah 31:7–14 Behold, I will bring them from the north country . . . the woman with child and her who is in travail together; a great company, they shall return here. I am a father to Israel, and Ephraim is my first-born.	Psalm 84:1–8 *or* **Refrain:** How dear to me is your dwelling, O Lord of hosts. *Psalm 84* 1bc,2/3,4/5,6/7,8

SECOND LESSON	CHANT BEFORE GOSPEL	GOSPEL

Gal. 3:23–25; 4:4–7

God sent forth his Son, born of a woman, born under the law, to redeem those who were under the law, so that we might receive adoption as sons.

Alleluia

(John 1:14)
We have seen his glory;* glory that is his as the Father's only Son.

John 1:1–18

To all who received him he gave power to become the children of God. The law was given through Moses; grace and truth came through Jesus Christ.

Romans 1:1–7

The Gospel of God which he promised beforehand through his prophets in the holy scriptures, the gospel concerning his Son, who was descended from David according to the flesh.

or **Phil. 2:9–13**

God has . . . bestowed on him the name which is above every name.

Alleluia

(Heb. 1:1,2)
In the past God spoke to our fathers through the prophets,* but now he has spoken to us through his Son.

Luke 2:15–21

At the end of eight days, when he was circumcised, he was called Jesus, the name given by the angel before he was conceived in the womb.

Eph. 1:3–6,15–19a

Blessed be the God and Father of our Lord Jesus Christ. He destined us in love to be his sons through Jesus Christ.

Alleluia

(John 1:14)
The Word was made flesh and dwelt among us,* full of grace and truth.

Matt. 2:13–15,19–23

Take the child and his mother. "Out of Egypt have I called my son."

or **Luke 2:41–52**

After three days they found him in the temple.

or **Matt. 2:1–12**

Wise men from the east came to Jerusalem, saying, Where is he who has been born king of the Jews?

	FIRST LESSON	PSALM
Year ABC The Epiphany January 6 Hymn 47	Isaiah 60:1–6,9 Nations shall come to your light, and kings to the brightness of your rising. They shall bring gold and frankincense.	Psalm 72:1–2,10–17 *or* **Refrain:** All kings shall bow down before him; all the nations shall do him service. *Psalm 72* 1,2/8,10/12,13/17
Year A 1 Epiphany (The Baptism of Our Lord) Hymn 545 Entrance Hymn 53	Isaiah 42:1–9 Behold my servant, whom I uphold, my chosen, in whom my soul delights; I have put my Spirit upon him.	Psalm 89:20–29 *or* **Refrain:** I have found David my servant; with my holy oil have I anointed him. *Psalm 89* 21,22/24,25/26,27/28,29
Year A 2 Epiphany Hymn 9	Isaiah 49:1–7 I will give you as a light to the nations, that my salvation may reach to the end of the earth.	Psalm 40:1–10 *or* **Refrain** (Heb. 10:7): Behold, I come to do your will, O God. *Psalm 40* 1,3/7,8/9,10

SECOND LESSON	CHANT BEFORE GOSPEL	GOSPEL
Eph. 3:1–12 Grace was given to preach to the Gentiles the unsearchable riches of Christ.	**Alleluia** (Matt. 2:2) We have seen his star in the east,* and have come to worship the Lord.	**Matthew 2:1–12** Wise men from the east came to Jerusalem, saying, Where is he who has been born king of the Jews? They offered him gifts, gold and frankincense and myrrh.
Acts 10:34–38 Good news of peace by Jesus Christ . . . beginning from Galilee after the baptism which John preached: How God anointed Jesus of Nazareth with the Holy Spirit.	**Alleluia** (Gal. 3:27) All of you who were baptized into Christ* have clothed yourselves with Christ.	**Matthew 3:13–17** When Jesus was baptized, he went up immediately from the water, and behold, the heavens were opened and he saw the Spirit of God descending. This is my beloved Son.
1 Cor. 1:1–9 I give thanks to God always for you because of the grace of God which was given you in Christ Jesus, that in every way you were enriched.	**Alleluia** (John 1:29) Behold the Lamb of God;* behold him who takes away the sin of the world.	**John 1:29–41** John saw Jesus coming toward him, and said, Behold the Lamb of God, who takes away the sin of the world!

The Gospel Lessons for the remaining Sundays after Epiphany present the beginnings of our Lord's ministry. During Year A they are chosen from the Gospel according to Matthew. The Old Testament lessons are selected to match the Gospels. The Epistles consist of a semi-continuous reading of 1 Corinthians which was introduced last Sunday.

SEE PAGES 202–205 FOR OTHER SUGGESTED HYMNS

	FIRST LESSON	PSALM
Year A	**Amos 3:1–8**	**Psalm 139:1–11**
3 Epiphany	The Lord God does nothing, without revealing his secret to his servants the prophets. The Lord God has spoken; who can but prophesy?	*or* **Refrain:** Lord, you have searched me out and known me. *Psalm 139* 1bc,2/6,7/8,9/10,11
Hymn 566 or 437 (tune 391)		
Year A	**Micah 6:1–8**	**Psalm 37:1–6**
4 Epiphany	Plead your case before the mountains. What does the Lord require of you but to do justice, and to love kindness, and to walk humbly with your God?	*or* **Refrain:** Put your trust in the Lord and do good. *Psalm 37* 1,2/3,4/5,6
Hymn 418		
Year A	**Habakkuk 3:2–6,17–19**	**Psalm 27:1–7**
5 Epiphany	Thy work, O Lord, do I fear. In the midst of the years renew it; in the midst of the years make it known; in wrath remember mercy. His brightness was like the light.	*or* **Refrain:** The Lord is my light and my salvation. *Psalm 27* 1cd,2/3,4/5,6/7,9
Hymn 258		

SECOND LESSON	CHANT BEFORE GOSPEL	GOSPEL
1 Cor. 1:10–17	**Alleluia**	**Matthew 4:12–23**
I appeal to you, brethren, by the name of our Lord Jesus Christ, that all of you agree and that there be no dissensions among you.	(Matt. 4:23) Jesus preached the Good News of the kingdom;* and healed every disease among the people.	When Jesus heard that John had been arrested he withdrew into Galilee . . . and from that time on Jesus began to preach, saying, Repent, for the kingdom of heaven is at hand.
1 Cor. 1:(18–25)26–31	**Alleluia**	**Matthew 5:1–12**
God chose what is weak in the world to shame the strong.	*Ad libitum* *(See page 206)*	Jesus went up on the mountain. Blessed are the poor in spirit, for theirs is the kingdom of heaven.
1 Cor. 2:1–11	**Alleluia**	**Matthew 5:13–20**
I decided to know nothing among you except Jesus Christ and him crucified.	*Ad libitum*	You are the light of the world. Think not that I have come to abolish the law and the prophets; I have come to fulfill them.

HYMNS	FIRST LESSON	PSALM
Year A 6 Epiphany Hymn 493	**Ecclesiasticus 15:11–20** It was the Lord who created man in the beginning, and he left him in the power of his own inclination. To act faithfully is a matter of your own choice.	**Psalm 119:9–16** *or* **Refrain:** Happy are they who walk in the law of the Lord. *Psalm 119* 9,10/11,12/13,14/15,16
Year A 7 Epiphany Hymn 396	**Leviticus 19:1–2,9–18** You shall be holy; for I the Lord your God am holy. You shall love your neighbor as yourself.	**Psalm 71:16–24** *or* **Refrain:** I will recall your righteousness, O Lord. *Psalm 71* 17,18/19,21/22,23
Year A 8 Epiphany Hymn 314 or 298	**Isaiah 49:8–18** They shall not hunger or thirst . . . for he who has pity on them will lead them. I will not forget you.	**Psalm 62:6–14** *or* **Refrain:** For God alone my soul in silence waits. *Psalm 62* 6,7/8,9/13,14
Year A Last Sunday After Epiphany (The Transfiguration) Hymn 119 Dismissal Hymn 54	**Exodus 24:12(13–14)15–18** Moses went up on the mountain, and the cloud covered the mountain. The glory of the Lord was like a devouring fire . . . in the sight of the people of Israel.	**Psalm 99** *or* **Refrain:** Proclaim the greatness of the Lord our God; he is the Holy One. *Psalm 99* 1,2/6,7/8,9

SECOND LESSON	CHANT BEFORE GOSPEL	GOSPEL
1 Cor. 3:1–9 I, brethren, could not address you as spiritual men. You were not ready. While there is jealousy and strife among you, are you not of the flesh?	**Alleluia** *Ad libitum*	**Matthew** **5:21–24,27–30,33–37** First be reconciled to your brother, and then come and offer your gift. If your right eye causes you to sin, pluck it out. Do not swear at all. Let what you say be simply Yes or No.
1 Cor. 3:10–11,16–23 You are God's temple . . . God's Spirit dwells in you. God's temple is holy, and that temple you are.	**Alleluia** *Ad libitum*	**Matthew 5:38–48** You have heard that it was said, You shall love your neighbor and hate your enemy. I say . . . Love your enemies.
1 Cor. 4:1–5(6–7)8–13 Do not pronounce judgment before the time, before the Lord comes, who will bring to light the things now hidden.	**Alleluia** *Ad libitum*	**Matthew 6:24–34** Do not be anxious, saying, What shall we eat? Your heavenly Father knows that you need them all. Seek first his kingdom . . . and all these things shall be yours as well.
Philippians 3:7–14 For his sake I have suffered the loss of all things . . . in order that I may gain Christ and be found in him.	**Alleluia** (Matt. 17:5) This is my Son, my Beloved,* with whom I am well pleased.	**Matthew 17:1–9** Jesus took with him Peter and James and John . . . and led them up a high mountain apart. And he was transfigured before them, and his face shone like the sun.

	FIRST LESSON	PSALM
Year ABC	**Joel 2:1–2,12–17**	**Psalm 103:8–14**
Ash Wednesday	Return to me with all your heart, with fasting, with weeping. Return to the Lord, your God, for he is gracious and merciful.	*or* **Refrain:** The Lord remembers that we are but dust. *Psalm 103* 8,9/10,11/12,13
Hymn 56 Dismissal Hymn 61		

or **Isaiah 58:1–12**
Cry aloud . . . declare to my people their transgression. Is not this the fast I choose: to loose the bonds of wickedness . . . to let the oppressed go free?

Proper Liturgy, page 264

2 Cor. 5:20b—6:10

Behold, now is the
acceptable time;
behold, now is the day
of salvation.

Verse*

(2 Cor. 6:2)
Behold, now is the
acceptable time;*
behold, now is the day
of salvation.

or **Tract**
Psalm 130:1–4(5–7)

* *See the Introduction*

Matt. 6:1–6,16–21

Beware of practicing
your piety before men
in order to be seen by
them; for then you will
have no reward from
your Father who is in
heaven.

The Lessons appointed for the Season of Lent are intended as background and preparation for Easter. The Old Testament Lessons present a synopsis of the history of salvation from Creation to the Captivity in Babylon. The Gospels, beginning with the Third Sunday, consist of the great Johannine Signs which illuminate the Church's understanding of Holy Baptism.

SEE PAGES 202-205 FOR OTHER SUGGESTED HYMNS	FIRST LESSON	PSALM
Year A 1 Lent (The Temptation of our Lord) Hymn 55	**Genesis 2:4b–9,15–17; 25—3:7** *The Fall from Grace* The Lord God formed man of dust from the ground. The tree of the knowledge of good and evil you shall not eat. The serpent said . . . You will not die. Your eyes will be opened, and you will be like God, knowing good and evil.	**Psalm 51:1–13** *or* **Refrain:** Have mercy on me, O God, according to your loving kindness. *Psalm 51* 2,3/4,5/6,7/8,9/10, 11/12,13
Year A 2 Lent Hymn 285	**Genesis 12:1–8** *The Call of Abraham* The Lord said to Abram, Go from your country. The Lord appeared to Abram and said, To your descendants I will give this land. He built there an altar to the Lord.	**Psalm 33:12–22** *or* **Refrain:** Lord, let your loving-kindness be upon us, as we have put our trust in you. *Psalm 33* 12,13/14,15/18,19/20,21

SECOND LESSON	CHANT BEFORE GOSPEL	GOSPEL
Romans **5:12–19(20–21)** Sin came into the world through one man and death through sin, and so death spread to all men because all men sinned.	**Verse** (Matt. 4:4) Man shall not live by bread alone,* but by every word that proceeds from the mouth of God. *or* **Tract** Psalm 91:1–4,9–11	**Matthew 4:1–11** Jesus was led up by the Spirit into the wilderness to be tempted by the devil.
Romans **4:1–5(6–12)13–17** The promise to Abraham and his descendants, that they should inherit the world, did not come through the law but through the righteousness of faith.	**Verse** (John 3:16) God so loved the world that he gave his only Son,* that all who believe in him might have eternal life. *or* **Tract** Psalm 106:1–5 *(Omit the initial Hallelujah)*	**John 3:1–17** *The Discourse with Nicodemus* God so loved the world that he gave his only Son, that whoever believes in him should not perish but have eternal life.

	FIRST LESSON	PSALM

Year A	**Exodus 17:1-7**	**Psalm 95:6-11**
3 Lent	*Water from the Rock*	*or* **Refrain** (Heb. 4:7): Today if you would hear his voice, harden not your hearts. *Psalm 95* 6,7/8,9/10,11
Hymn 434	There was no water for the people to drink. The Lord said to Moses, Pass on before the people . . . take in your hand the rod. I will stand before you. You shall strike the rock, and water shall come out of it.	

Year A	**1 Samuel 16:1-13**	**Psalm 23**
4 Lent	*The Anointing of David*	*or* **Refrain:** The Lord is my shepherd; I shall not be in want. *Psalm 23* 2,3/4ab,4cd/5,6
Hymn 61 Entrance Hymn 597 Dismissal Hymn 584	The Lord said to Samuel . . . Fill your horn with oil. I will send you to Jesse the Bethlehemite, for I have provided for myself a king among his sons. Samuel took the horn of oil, and anointed him.	

Year A	**Ezekiel 37:1-3(4-10)11-14**	**Psalm 130**
5 Lent	*The Valley of Dry Bones*	*or* **Refrain:** With the Lord there is mercy; with him there is plenteous redemption. *Psalm 130* 1/2,3/4,5/6,7
Hymn 71	The hand of the Lord was upon me . . . and set me down in the midst of the valley; it was full of bones. Son of man, can these bones live?	

SECOND LESSON	CHANT BEFORE GOSPEL	GOSPEL
Romans 5:1–11 Since we are justified by faith, we have peace with God through our Lord Jesus Christ.	**Verse** (John 4:42,15) Lord, you are truly the Savior of the world;* give me living water that I may never thirst again. *or* **Tract** Psalm 42:1–7	**John** **4:5–26(27–38)39–42** *The Woman at the Well* Every one who drinks of this water will thirst again, but whoever drinks of the water that I shall give him will never thirst; the water that I shall give him will become in him a spring of water welling up to eternal life.
Eph. 5:(1–7)8–14 Once you were darkness, but now you are light in the Lord; walk as children of light.	**Verse** (John 8:12) I am the light of the world, says the Lord;* whoever follows me will have the light of life. *or* **Tract** Psalm 122:(1–5)6–9	**John** **9:1–13(14–27)28–38** *The Man Born Blind* Rabbi, who sinned, this man or his parents? Jesus answered, It was not that this man sinned, or his parents, but that the works of God might be made manifest in him. I am the light of the world.
Romans 6:16–23 The wages of sin is death, but the free gift of God is eternal life in Christ Jesus our Lord.	**Verse** (John 11:25,26) I am the resurrection and the life, says the Lord;* whoever believes in me shall not die for ever. *or* **Tract** Psalm 129:1–4(5–8)	**John 11:(1–16)17–44** *The Raising of Lazarus* Jesus cried with a loud voice, Lazarus, come out. The dead man came out.

*Liturgy of the Psalms: Page 270. Gospel of the Palms:
Matthew 21:1–11. At the Procession: Hymn 62 & Psalm 118:19–29.
Refrain after each verse of the Psalm: Hosanna in the highest.*

SEE PAGES 202–205 FOR
OTHER SUGGESTED
HYMNS

	FIRST LESSON	PSALM
Year A	**Isaiah 45:21–25**	**Psalm 22:1–11**
The Sunday of The Passion	Turn to me and be saved. To me every knee shall bow.	*or* **Refrain:** My God, my God, why have you forsaken me?
or		*Psalm 22* 1,2,3/4,5,6/7,8,9/10,11
Palm Sunday	*or* **Isaiah 52:13—53:12** He has borne our griefs. He was wounded for our transgressions.	
Hymn 68 or 67 Dismissal Hymn 75		
Year ABC	**Isaiah 42:1–9**	**Psalm 36:5–10**
Monday in Holy Week	*First Song of the Servant of Yahweh*	*or* **Refrain:** In your light, O God, we see light.
Hymn 69	Behold my servant, whom I uphold, my chosen, in whom my soul delights; I have put my Spirit upon him, he will bring forth justice to the nations.	*Psalm 36* 5,6/7,8/9,10

SECOND LESSON	CHANT BEFORE GOSPEL	GOSPEL
Philippians 2:5–11 He humbled himself and became obedient unto death . . . that at the name of Jesus every knee should bow.	**Verse** (Phil. 2:8,9) Christ for us became obedient unto death, even death on a cross;* therefore God has highly exalted him and bestowed on him the name which is above every name. *or* **Tract** Psalm 22:26–30	**Matthew** **26:36—27:54(55–66)** *or* **Matthew** **27:1–54(55–66)** *The Passion of our Lord Jesus Christ*
Hebrews 11:39—12:3 Looking to Jesus . . . who for the joy that was set before him endured the cross, despising the shame, and is seated at the right hand of the throne of God.	**Verse** We adore you, O Christ, and we bless you,* because by your holy cross you have redeemed the world. *or* **Tract** Psalm 102:1–4, 12–13	**John 12:1–11** Six days before the Passover, Jesus came to Bethany. Mary took a pound of costly ointment . . . and anointed the feet of Jesus. *or* **Mark 14:3–9** She has anointed my body beforehand for burying. And truly, I say to you . . . what she has done will be told in memory of her.

	FIRST LESSON	PSALM
Year ABC Tuesday in Holy Week Hymn 73	**Isaiah 49:1–6** *Second Song of the Servant of Yahweh* It is too light a thing that you should be my servant to raise up the tribes of Jacob and to restore the preserved of Israel; I will give you as a light to the nations, that my salvation may reach to the end of the earth.	**Psalm 71:1–12** *or* **Refrain:** I have taken refuge in you, O Lord. *Psalm 71* 5,6/7,8/9,10
Year ABC Wednesday in Holy Week Hymn 81	**Isaiah 50:4–9a** *Third Song of the Servant of Yahweh* I gave my back to the smiters, and my cheeks to those who pulled out the beard; I hid not my face from shame and spitting.	**Psalm 69:7–15,22–23** *or* **Refrain:** Answer me, O God, in your great mercy. *Psalm 69* 7,8/9,10/14,15/22,23
Year ABC Maundy Thursday (The Lord's Supper) Hymn 195	**Exodus 12:1–14a** This month shall be for you the beginning of months. They shall take every man a lamb . . . a lamb for a household. It is the Lord's passover.	**Psalm 78:14–20,23–25** *or* **Refrain:** Mortals ate the bread of angels, for the Lord gave them manna from heaven. *Psalm 78* 14,15/17,18/19,23/24,25

Proper Liturgy, page 274

SECOND LESSON	CHANT BEFORE GOSPEL	GOSPEL
1 Cor. 1:18–31 The word of the cross is folly to those who are perishing, but to us who are being saved it is the power of God.	**Verse or Tract** *As on Monday*	**John 12:37–38,42–50** Jesus said, He who believes in me, believes not in me but in him who sent me. *or* **Mark 11:15–19** Jesus entered the temple and began to drive out those who sold and those who bought. Is it not written, "My house shall be called a house of prayer for all the nations?"
Heb. 9:11–15,24–28 When Christ appeared as a high priest of the good things that have come . . . he entered once for all into the Holy Place, taking . . . his own blood, thus securing an eternal redemption.	**Verse or Tract** *As on Monday*	**John 13:21–35** Jesus testified, Truly, truly, I say to you, one of you will betray me. *or* **Matt. 26:1–5,14–25** Judas went to the chief priests and said, What will you give me if I deliver him to you?
1 Corinthians 11:23–26(27–32) This is my body. This cup is the new covenant in my blood. Do this in remembrance of me.	**Verse** (John 13:34) A new commandment I give to you:* love one another as I have loved you. *or* **Tract** Psalm 43	**John 13:1–15** Jesus began to wash the disciples' feet. *or* **Luke 22:14–30** Jesus took a cup, and . . . said, Take this, and divide it. He took bread, and broke it, saying, This is my body.

Hymns 199 and 200 may appropriately be sung after the postcommunion prayer.

	FIRST LESSON	PSALM
Year ABC	**Isaiah 52:13—53:12**	**Psalm 22:1–11**
Good Friday	*Fourth Song of the Servant of Yahweh* He was wounded for our transgressions . . . He was numbered with the transgressors.	*or* **Refrain:** My God, my God, why have you forsaken me? *Psalm 22* 1,2/7,8/14,15/16,17/18, 19/20,21
Hymn 75		
	or **Genesis 22:1–18** You have not withheld your son, your only son.	
	or **Wisdom 2:1,12–24** If the righteous man is God's son, he will help him. Let us condemn him to a shameful death.	
Proper Liturgy, page 276		
Year ABC	**Job 14:1–14**	**Psalm 31:1–5**
Holy Saturday	If a man die, shall he live again?	*or* **Refrain** (Luke 23:46): Father, into your hands I commend my spirit. *Psalm 31* 1,2/3,4/5,16
Hymn 83		
Proper Liturgy, page 283		

Hebrews 10:1–25

"A body hast thou prepared for me." By a single offering he has perfected for all time those who are sanctified. There is no longer any offering for sin.

Verse

(Phil. 2:8,9)
Christ for us became obedient unto death, even death on a cross;* therefore God has highly exalted him and bestowed on him the name which is above every name.

or **Tract**
Psalm 40:1–14
or Psalm 69:1–10, 14–23

John (18:1–40); 19:1–37

The Passion of our Lord Jesus Christ

It is finished.

---

1 Peter 4:1–8

The Gentiles will give account to him who is ready to judge the living and the dead. This is why the gospel was preached even to the dead.

Verse

We adore you, O Christ, and we bless you,* because by your holy cross you have redeemed the world.

or **Tract**
Psalm 130

Matthew 27:57–66

or **John 19:38–42**

The Burial of our Lord Jesus Christ

The Great Vigil of Easter: Liturgy of the Word.

At least two of the following Lessons are read, of which one is always the Lesson from Exodus. Four or five Lessons are customary. After each Lesson, the Psalm or Canticle listed, or some other suitable psalm, canticle, or hymn may be sung. A period of silence may be kept, and the Collect provided, or some other suitable Collect may be said. The entire Great Vigil of Easter may be found on pages 284–285 of the Prayer Book.

1. **Genesis 1:1—2:2**

   The Story of Creation

   Psalm 33:1–11
   or **Psalm 36:5–10**

   or
   Refrain: By the word of the Lord were the heavens made, by the breath of his mouth all the heavenly hosts.
   Psalm 33
   1,2/3,4/5,7/8,9/10,11

   or
   Refrain: In your light, O God, we see light.
   Psalm 36
   5,6/7,8/9,10

2. **Genesis 7:1–5,11–18; 8:6–18; 9:8–13**

   The Flood

   Psalm 46

   or
   Refrain: The Lord of hosts is with us; the God of Jacob is our stronghold.
   Psalm 46
   1,2,3/5,6,7/9,10,11

3. **Genesis 22:1–18**

   Abraham's sacrifice of Isaac

   Psalm 33:12–22
   or **Psalm 16**

   or
   Refrain: Happy is the nation whose God is the Lord.
   Psalm 33
   13,14,15/16,18,19/20,21,22

   or
   Refrain: Protect me, O God, for I take refuge in you.
   Psalm 16
   5,6/8,9/10,11

4. **Exodus 14:10—15:1**

   Israel's deliverance at the Red Sea

   Canticle 8, The Song of Moses

   or
   Refrain: I will sing to the Lord, for he has risen up in might.
   Canticle 8
   1,2/3,4/5,6/7,8/9,10/11,12,13

5. Isaiah 4:2–6

*God's Presence in a
Renewed Israel*

Psalm 122

or
Refrain: Pray for the peace of Jerusalem.
Psalm 122
1,2/3,4/6,7/8,9

6. Isaiah 55:1–11

*Salvation offered freely to
all*

Canticle 9, The First Song of Isaiah

or
Refrain: You shall draw water with rejoicing
from the springs of salvation.
Canticle 9
1,2/4,5/6,7

7. Ezekiel 36:24–28

*A new heart and a new
spirit*

Psalm 42:1–7

or
Refrain: As the deer longs for the water-brooks,
so longs my soul for you, O God.
Psalm 42
2,3/4,5/6,7

8. Ezekiel 37:1–14

The valley of dry bones

Psalm 30
or **Psalm 143**

or
Refrain: You brought me up, O Lord, from the
dead.
Psalm 30
1,2,3/4,5,6/12,13

or
Refrain: Revive me, O Lord, for your Name's
sake.
Psalm 143
1,2/4,5/6,7/8,10

9. Zephaniah 3:12–20

*The gathering of God's
people*

Psalm 98
or **Psalm 126**

or
Refrain: Shout with joy to the Lord, all you
lands; lift up your voice, rejoice, and sing.
Psalm 98
1,2/3,4/6,7/8,9

or
Refrain: The Lord has done great things for us,
and we are glad indeed.
Psalm 126
1,2/3,4/5,6/7

Year ABC Easter Day At the Vigil or Early Service	*After the Collect of the Vigil Eucharist, continue with the Epistle.* *At an early Service, use one of the Old Testament Lessons from the Vigil followed by the corresponding Psalm or Canticle.*	

Year A Easter Day Principal Service Hymn 97	**Acts 10:34–43** God raised him on the third day and made him manifest. *or* **Exodus 14:10–14,21–25; 15:20–21** The people of Israel went into the midst of the sea on dry ground.	**Psalm 118:14–17,22–24** *or* **Refrain:** On this day the Lord has acted; we will rejoice and be glad in it. *Psalm 118* 14,15/16,17/22,23

Year ABC Easter Day Evening Service Hymn 207	**Acts 5:29a,30–32** The God of our fathers raised Jesus whom you killed by hanging him on a tree. *or* **Daniel 12:1–3** Many of those who sleep in the dust of the earth shall awake, some to everlasting life, and some to shame and everlasting contempt.	**Psalm 114** *or* **Psalm 118:14–17,22–24** *or* **Psalm 136** *or* **Refrain:** Hallelujah! *Psalm 114* 1,2/3,4/5,6/7,8 *or Psalm 118 as at the principal service*

[28]

SECOND LESSON	CHANT BEFORE GOSPEL	GOSPEL
Romans 6:3–11 All of us who have been baptized into Christ Jesus were baptized into his death . . . so that as Christ was raised . . . we too might walk in newness of life.	**Alleluia** V. Alleluia. R. Alleluia. *Repeated three times, followed by:* **Refrain:** Hallelujah! *Psalm 114* 1,2/3,4/5,6/7,8 *If preferred the Psalm may be sung without Refrain.*	**Matthew 28:1–10** After the sabbath, toward the dawn of the first day of the week . . . He is not here; for he has risen. *Offertory Hymn:* 89
Colossians 3:1–4 You have been raised with Christ. For you have died, and your life is hid with Christ in God. *or* **Acts 10:34–43**	**Alleluia** (1 Cor. 5:7,8) Christ our Passover is sacrificed for us:* therefore let us keep the feast.	**John 20:1–10,(11–18)** Mary Magdalene came to the tomb . . . and saw that the stone had been taken away. She went to Simon Peter . . . They have taken the Lord out of the tomb. *or* **Matt. 28:1–10** *(as at the Vigil)*
1 Cor. 5:6b–8 Christ, our paschal lamb, has been sacrificed. Let us, therefore, celebrate the festival, not with the old leaven, the leaven of malice and evil, but with the unleavened bread of sincerity and truth. *or* **Acts 5:29a,30–32**	**Alleluia** *As at the Morning Service*	**Luke 24:13–35** That very day two of them were going to a village named Emmaus . . . When he was at table with them, he took the bread and blessed, and broke it, and gave it to them. And their eyes were opened and they recognized him.

Year ABC	**Acts 2:14,22b–32**	**Psalm 16:8–11** *or* **Psalm 118:19–24**
Monday in Easter Week	Peter addressed them.	
	This Jesus, delivered up	*or*
Hymn 91	according to the	**Refrain:** Hallelujah!
	definite plan and	*Psalm 16*
	foreknowledge of God,	8/9/10/11
	you crucified and killed	
	by the hands of lawless	*or*
	men. But God raised	**Refrain:** Give thanks to
	him up. Of that we all	the Lord, for he is good;
	are witnesses.	his mercy endures for
		ever.
		or Hallelujah!
		Psalm 118
		19,20/21,22/23,24

Year ABC	**Acts 2:36–41**	**Psalm 33:18–22**
Tuesday in Easter Week	Let all the house of	*or*
Hymn 100	Israel therefore know	**Refrain:** Hallelujah!
(Tune 113)	assuredly that God has	*Psalm 33*
	made him both Lord	1,2/18,19/20,21
	and Christ. Repent,	
	and be baptized.	*or Psalm 118 as on*
		Monday

Year ABC	**Acts 3:1–10**	**Psalm 105:1–8**
Wednesday in Easter	Peter said, I have no	*or*
Week	silver and gold, but I	**Refrain:** Hallelujah!
	give you what I have; in	*Psalm 105*
Hymn 207	the name of Jesus	1,2/3,4/5,6/7,8
	Christ of Nazareth,	
	walk.	*or Psalm 118 as on*
		Monday

*In place of the Psalm,
an Alleluia Verse may
be used.*

Alleluia

(Psalm 118:24)
On this day the Lord
has acted;* we will
rejoice and be glad in
it.

Matthew 28:9–15

When the chief priests
had assembled with the
elders and taken
counsel, they gave a
sum of money to the
soldiers and said, Tell
people, "His disciples
came by night and stole
him away while we
were asleep."

Alleluia

As on Monday

John 20:11–18

Mary Magdelene saw
Jesus standing, but she
did not know that it was
Jesus. Supposing him to
be the gardener, she
said to him, Sir, if you
have carried him away,
tell me where. Jesus
said to her, Mary. She
turned and said to him
in Hebrew, Rabboni!

Alleluia

As on Monday

Luke 24:13–35

Two of the disciples
were going to . . .
Emmaus. When he was
at table with them, he
took the bread and
blessed, and broke it,
and gave it to them.
Their eyes were opened
and they recognized
him.

	FIRST LESSON	PSALM

Year ABC

Thursday in Easter
Week

Hymn 94

Acts 3:11–26

Peter addressed the
people. You denied the
Holy and Righteous
One, and asked for a
murderer to be granted
to you, and killed the
Author of life, whom
God raised from the
dead.

Psalm 8
or **Psalm 114**

or
Refrain: Hallelujah!
Psalm 8
1,2/4,5/6,7

or
Refrain: Hallelujah!
Psalm 114
1,2/3,4/5,6/7,8

*or Psalm 118 as on
Monday*

Year ABC

Friday in Easter Week

Hymn 437
(Tune 391)

Acts 4:1–12

The priests and the
captain of the temple
and the Sadducees
arrested them. Peter,
filled with the Holy
Spirit, said, Rulers . . .
be it known to you all
. . . that by the name
of Jesus Christ . . . this
man is standing before
you well.

Psalm 116:1–8

or
Refrain: Hallelujah!
Psalm 116
1/2,3/5,6/7,8

*or Psalm 118 as on
Monday*

Year ABC

Saturday in Easter
Week

Hymn 98

Acts 4:13–21

They saw the boldness
of Peter and John . . .
and charged them not
to speak. Peter and
John answered them
. . . We cannot but
speak of what we have
seen and heard.

Psalm 118:14–18

or
Refrain: Hallelujah!
Psalm 118
1,14/15,16/17,18

*or Psalm 118 as on
Monday*

In place of the Psalm, an Alleluia Verse may be used.	**Alleluia** *As on Monday*	**Luke 24:36b–48** Jesus himself stood among them. But they were startled and frightened, and supposed that they saw a spirit. See my hands and my feet, that it is I myself; handle me and see. Then he opened their minds to understand the scriptures.
	Alleluia *As on Monday*	**John 21:1–14** Jesus revealed himself again to the disciples by the Sea of Tiberias. He said, Cast the net on the right side of the boat. Peter . . . hauled the net ashore, full of large fish, a hundred and fifty-three of them.
	Alleluia *As on Monday*	**Mark 16:9–15,20** When Jesus rose early on the first day of the week, he appeared to Mary Magdelene. Afterward he appeared to the eleven. He upbraided them for their unbelief and hardness of heart, because they had not believed those who saw him. Go into all the world and preach the gospel.

In Easter Season a Reading from the Acts of the Apostles normally takes the place of an Old Testament Lesson.

SEE PAGES 202–205 FOR OTHER SUGGESTED HYMNS

	FIRST LESSON	PSALM
Year A 2 of Easter (The Sunday of Thomas) Hymn 99	**Acts 2:14a,22–32** Peter addressed them. God raised Jesus up, having loosed the pangs of death, because it was not possible for him to be held by it. *or* **Gen. 8:6–16; 9:8–16** God said to Noah . . . I establish my covenant with you . . . never again shall there be a flood to destroy the earth.	**Psalm 118:19–24** *or* **Psalm 111** *or* **Refrain:** Give thanks to the Lord, for he is good; his mercy endures for ever. *or* Hallelujah! *Psalm 118* 19,20/21,22/23,24 *or* **Refrain:** Hallelujah! *Psalm 111* 1,2/3,4/9,10
Year A 3 of Easter Hymn 89	**Acts 2:14a,36–47** Peter said to them, Repent, and be baptized. They devoted themselves . . . to the breaking of bread and the prayers. *or* **Isaiah 43:1–12** Thus says the Lord: I have redeemed you. I am the Lord your God, the Holy One of Israel.	**Psalm 116:10–17** *or* **Refrain:** I will walk in the presence of the Lord in the land of the living. *or* Hallelujah! *Psalm 116* 10,11/12,13/14,15/16,17

The Gospels for the first three Sundays of Easter present the principal resurrection narratives. Good Shepherd Sunday is now the fourth Sunday of the season. The rest of the Sundays of Easter take their Gospels from the Johannine discourses.

SECOND LESSON	CHANT BEFORE GOSPEL	GOSPEL
1 Peter 1:3–9	**Alleluia**	**John 20:19–31**
We have been born anew to a living hope through the resurrection of Jesus Christ from the dead. *or* **Acts 2:14a,22–32**	(John 20:29) You believe in me, Thomas, because you have seen me;* blessed are those who have not seen and yet believe.	The first day of the week . . . Receive the Holy Spirit. Eight days later . . . Blessed are those who have not seen and yet believe.
1 Peter 1:17–23	**Alleluia**	**Luke 24:13–35**
You were ransomed from the futile ways inherited from your fathers . . . with the precious blood of Christ. *or* **Acts 2:14a,36–47**	(Luke 24:32) Open our minds, O Lord, to understand the Scriptures;* make our hearts burn within us when you speak.	Two of the disciples were going to Emmaus. When he was at table with them, he took the bread and blessed, and broke it, and gave it to them. Their eyes were opened and they recognized him.

	FIRST LESSON	PSALM
Year A 4 of Easter (The Good Shepherd) Hymn 345	**Acts 6:1–9; 7:2a,51–60** Stephen . . . did great wonders. As they were stoning Stephen he prayed, Lord Jesus, receive my spirit. *or* **Neh. 9:6–15** Thou didst tell them to go in to possess the land which thou hadst sworn to give them.	**Psalm 23** *or* **Refrain:** The Lord is my shepherd; I shall not be in want. *Psalm 23* 2,3/4ab,4cd/5,6 *or* **Refrain:** Hallelujah! *Psalm 23* 1,2/3,4/5,6
Year A 5 of Easter Hymn 361	**Acts 17:1–15** Paul argued with them from the scriptures. This Jesus . . . is the Christ. Some were persuaded. But the Jews were jealous. *or* **Deut. 6:20–25** We were Pharaoh's slaves in Egypt, and the Lord brought us out.	**Psalm 66:1–8** *or* **Refrain:** Be joyful in God, all you lands. *or* Hallelujah! *Psalm 66* 1,2/3,4/5,6/7,8

[36]

SECOND LESSON	CHANT BEFORE GOSPEL	GOSPEL
1 Peter 2:19–25 You were straying like sheep, but you have now returned to the Shepherd and Guardian of your souls. *or* **Acts 6:1–9; 7:2a,51–60**	**Alleluia** (John 10:14) I am the good shepherd, says the Lord;* I know my sheep, and my sheep know me.	**John 10:1–10** He who enters by the door is the shepherd of the sheep.
1 Peter 2:1–10 Come to him, to that living stone . . . and like living stones be yourselves built into a spiritual house, to be a holy priesthood. *or* **Acts 17:1–15**	**Alleluia** (John 14:6) I am the way, the truth, and the life;* no one comes to the Father, but by me.	**John 14:1–14** Let not your hearts be troubled . . . I go to prepare a place for you. I am the way, and the truth, and the life.

	FIRST LESSON	PSALM
Year A	Acts 17:22–31	Psalm 148:7–14
6 of Easter	Paul said, Men of	*or*
Hymn 380	Athens . . . the God	**Refrain** (Ps. 149:1):
	who made the world	Sing to the Lord a new
	and everything in it,	song.
	being Lord of heaven	*or* Hallelujah!
	and earth . . . gives to	*Psalm 148*
	all men life and breath	7,8/9,10/11,12/13,14
	and everything.	
	or **Isaiah 41:17–20**	
	I will make the	
	wilderness a pool of	
	water. I will put in the	
	wilderness the cedar	
Entrance Hymn 376	. . . that men may see	
	and know . . . that the	
	hand of the Lord has	
	done this.	
Year A	Acts 1:1–11	Psalm 110:1–5
		or Psalm 47
Ascension Day	Men of Galilee, why do	
	you stand looking into	*or*
Hymn 104	heaven?	**Refrain** (Matt. 28:20): I
		am with you always, to
	or **Daniel 7:9–14**	the close of the age.
	To him was given	*or* Hallelujah!
	dominion . . . which	*Psalm 110*
	shall not pass away.	1/2/3/4
		or
		Refrain: God has gone
		up with a shout, the
		Lord with the sound of
		the ram's-horn.
		or Hallelujah!
		Psalm 47
		1,2/5,6/7,8

SECOND LESSON	CHANT BEFORE GOSPEL	GOSPEL
1 Peter 3:8–18 Have unity of spirit, sympathy, love of the brethren. Be prepared to make a defense to any one who calls you to account for the hope that is in you. *or* **Acts 17:22–31**	**Alleluia** (John 15:4,5) Abide in me as I in you, says the Lord;* I am the vine and you are the branches.	**John 15:1–8** As the branch cannot bear fruit by itself, unless it abides in the vine, neither can you unless you abide in me.
Ephesians 1:15–23 The riches of his glorious inheritance in the saints . . . which he accomplished in Christ when he raised him from the dead. *or* **Acts 1:1–11**	**Alleluia** (Matt. 28:19,20) Go and make disciples of all nations;* I am with you always, to the close of the age.	**Luke 24:49–53** While he blessed them, he parted from them, and was carried up into heaven. *or* **Mark 16:9–15,19–20** The Lord Jesus . . . was taken up into heaven, and sat down at the right hand of God.

	FIRST LESSON	PSALM
Year A 7 of Easter Hymn 106	**Acts 1:(1–7)8–14** You shall receive power when the Holy Spirit has come upon you; and you shall be my witnesses. *or* **Ezekiel 39:21–29** I will not hide my face any more from them, when I pour out my Spirit upon the house of Israel, says the Lord God.	**Psalm 47** *or* **Psalm 68:1–20** *or* **Refrain:** God has gone up with a shout, the Lord with the sound of the ram's-horn. *or* Hallelujah! *Psalm 47* 1,2/5,6/7,8 *or* **Refrain:** Sing to God, O kingdoms of the earth; sing praises to the Lord. *or* Hallelujah! *Psalm 68* 4,5/7,8/17,18

1 Peter 4:12–19	Alleluia	John 17:1–11
If one suffers as a Christian, let him not be ashamed, but under that name let him glorify God. *or* Acts 1:(1–7)8–14	(John 14:18) The Lord said, I will not leave you desolate;* I will come back to you, and your hearts will rejoice.	Father, glorify thou me in thy own presence with the glory which I had with thee before the world was made. Now I am no more in the world, but they are in the world. Keep them in thy name.

	FIRST LESSON	PSALM
Year ABC Vigil of Pentecost or Early Service	**Genesis 11:1–9** *The Tower of Babel*	**Psalm 33:12–22** *or* **Refrain:** Happy is the nation whose God is the Lord. *Psalm 33* 13,14,15/16,18,19/20,21, 22
	Exodus 19:1–9,16–20a; 20:18–20 *The Covenant*	**Canticle 2 or 13** *or* **Refrain:** (Exod. 19:6) He has made us a kingdom of priests and a holy nation. *Canticle 13* 1,2/3,4/5,6
	Ezekiel 37:1–14 *The valley of dry bones*	**Psalm 130** *or* **Refrain:** With the Lord there is mercy; with him there is plenteous redemption. *Psalm 130* 1/2,3/4,5/6,7
	Joel 2:28–32 *God will pour out his Spirit.*	**Canticle 9** *or* **Refrain:** You shall draw water with rejoicing from the springs of salvation. *Canticle 9* 1,2/4,5/6,7
	Acts 2:1–11 *The story of Pentecost*	**Psalm 104:25–32** *or* **Refrain:** Send forth your Spirit, O Lord, and renew the face of the earth. *or* Hallelujah! *Psalm 104* 25,26/28,29/30,31/32,35

Romans 8:14–17,22–27

All who are led by the Spirit of God are sons of God.

or **Acts 2:1–11**

Alleluia

Come, Holy Spirit, and fill the hearts of your faithful people,* and kindle in them the fire of your love.

John 7:37–39a

If any one thirst, let him come to me and drink. This he said about the Spirit.

It is appropriate that the Gospel be read several times, each time in a different language.

	FIRST LESSON	PSALM

Year A The Day of Pentecost Principal Service Hymn 109	**Acts 2:1–11** When the day of Pentecost had come, they were all together in one place. *or* **Ezek. 1:17–20** I will give them one heart, and put a new spirit within them.	**Psalm 104:25–32** *or* **Psalm 33:12–15,18–22** *or* **Refrain:** Send forth your Spirit, O Lord, and renew the face of the earth. *or* Hallelujah! *Psalm 104* 25,26/28,29/30,31/32,35

Year A Trinity Sunday Hymn 266	**Genesis 1:1—2:3** In the beginning God created the heavens and the earth. The Spirit of God was moving over the face of the waters.	**Canticle 2 or 13** *or* **Psalm 150** *or* **Refrain:** Glory to you, Father, Son, and Holy Spirit. *Canticle 13* 1,2/3,4/5,6 *or* **Refrain:** Let everything that has breath praise the Lord. *Psalm 150* 1,2/3,4/5,6

SECOND LESSON	CHANT BEFORE GOSPEL	GOSPEL
1 Cor. 12:4–13 To each is given the manifestation of the Spirit for the common good. *or* Acts 2:1–11	Alleluia Come, Holy Spirit, and fill the hearts of your faithful people,* and kindle in them the fire of your love.	John 20:19–23 Receive the Holy Spirit. If you forgive the sins of any, they are forgiven. *or* John 14:8–17 If you love me, you will keep my commandments. And I will pray the Father, and he will give you another Counselor, to be with you for ever.
2 Cor. 13:(5–10)11–14 The grace of the Lord Jesus Christ and the love of God and the fellowship of the Holy Spirit be with you all.	Alleluia (Rev. 1:4) Glory to the Father and to the Son and to the Holy Spirit:* to God who is, and who was, and who is to come.	Matthew 28:16–20 Make disciples of all nations, baptizing them in the name of the Father and of the Son and of the Holy Spirit.

The Gospels for the Sundays after Pentecost in Year A continue the reading of the Gospel according to Matthew begun on the Sundays after Epiphany. The Second Lessons consist of semi-continuous readings from the Pauline Epistles. The Old Testament Lessons are chosen to match the Gospel (or, occasionally, the Epistle).

SEE PAGES 202–205 FOR OTHER SUGGESTED HYMNS	FIRST LESSON	PSALM
Year A Proper 1 Closest to May 11 Hymn 493	**Ecclesiasticus 15:11–20** It was the Lord who created man in the beginning, and he left him in the power of his own inclination. To act faithfully is a matter of your own choice.	**Psalm 119:9–16** or **Refrain:** Happy are they who walk in the law of the Lord. *Psalm 119* 9,10/11,12/13,14/15,16
Year A Proper 2 Closest to May 18 Hymn 396	**Leviticus 19:1–2,9–18** You shall be holy; for I the Lord your God am holy. You shall love your neighbor as yourself.	**Psalm 71:16–24** or **Refrain:** I will recall your righteousness, O Lord. *Psalm 71* 17,18/19,21/22,23
Year A Proper 3 Closest to May 25 Hymn 314 or 192	**Isaiah 49:8–18** They shall not hunger or thirst . . . for he who has pity on them will lead them. I will not forget you.	**Psalm 62:6–14** or **Refrain:** For God alone my soul in silence waits. *Psalm 62* 6,7/8,9/13,14

SECOND LESSON	CHANT BEFORE GOSPEL	GOSPEL
1 Cor. 3:1–9	**Alleluia**	**Matthew** 5:21–24,27–30,33–37
I, brethren, could not address you as spiritual men. You were not ready. While there is jealousy and strife among you, are you not of the flesh?	*Ad libitum* *(See page 206)*	First be reconciled to your brother, and then come and offer your gift. If your right eye causes you to sin, pluck it out. Do not swear at all. Let what you say be simply Yes or No.
1 Cor. 3:10–11,16–23	**Alleluia**	**Matthew 5:38–48**
You are God's temple . . . God's Spirit dwells in you. God's temple is holy, and that temple you are.	*Ad libitum*	You have heard that it was said, You shall love your neighbor and hate your enemy. I say . . . Love your enemies.
1 Cor. 4:1–5(6–7)8–13	**Alleluia**	**Matthew 6:24–34**
Do not pronounce judgment before the time, before the Lord comes, who will bring to light the things now hidden.	*Ad libitum*	Do not be anxious, saying, what shall we eat? Your heavenly Father knows that you need them all. Seek first his kingdom . . . and all these things shall be yours as well.

	FIRST LESSON	PSALM
Year A Proper 4 Closest to June 1 Hymn 402	**Deut. 11:18–21,26–28** Behold, I set before you this day a blessing and a curse: the blessing, if you obey the commandments of the Lord your God, which I command you this day, and the curse, if you do not obey the commandments.	**Psalm 31:1–5,19–24** *or* **Refrain:** Into your hands I commend my spirit. *Psalm 31* 1,2/3,4/5,16
Year A Proper 5 Closest to June 8 Hymn 522	**Hosea 5:15—6:6** I desire steadfast love and not sacrifice, the knowledge of God, rather than burnt offerings.	**Psalm 50:7–15** *or* **Refrain:** To those who keep in my way will I show the salvation of God. *Psalm 50* 7,8/9,10/12,13/14,15
Year A Proper 6 Closest to June 15 Hymn 131 or 253	**Exodus 19:2–8a** I bore you on eagles' wings and brought you to myself. Now therefore, if you . . . keep my covenant you shall be to me a kingdom of priests and a holy nation.	**Psalm 100** *or* **Refrain:** We are his people and the sheep of his pasture. *Psalm 100* 1/2/3/4

SECOND LESSON	CHANT BEFORE GOSPEL	GOSPEL
Romans 3:21–25a,28 Since all have sinned and fall short of the glory of God, they are justified by his grace as a gift, through the redemption which is in Christ Jesus.	**Alleluia** *Ad libitum*	**Matthew 7:21–27** Not everyone who says to me, Lord, Lord, shall enter the kingdom of heaven, but he who does the will of my Father who is in heaven.
Romans 4:13–18 The promise to Abraham and his descendants, that they should inherit the world, did not come through the law but through the righteousness of faith.	**Alleluia** *Ad libitum*	**Matthew 9:9–13** Go and learn what this means. I desire mercy and not sacrifice. For I came not to call the righteous, but sinners.
Romans 5:6–11 God shows his love for us in that while we were yet sinners Christ died for us.	**Alleluia** *Ad libitum*	**Matthew 9:35—10:8(9–15)** Go nowhere among the Gentiles . . . go rather to the lost sheep of the house of Israel.

	FIRST LESSON	PSALM
Year A Proper 7 Closest to June 22 Hymn 343	**Jeremiah 20:7–13** The Lord is with me as a dread warrior; therefore my persecutors will stumble.	**Psalm 69:7–10,16–18** *or* **Refrain:** Answer me, O God, in your great mercy. *Psalm 69* 7,8/9,10/16,18
Year A Proper 8 Closest to June 29 Hymn 284	**Isaiah 2:10–17** Enter into the rock, and hide in the dust and from before the terror of the Lord, and from the glory of his majesty. The Lord alone will be exalted in that day.	**Psalm 89:1–4,15–18** *or* **Refrain:** Your love, O Lord, for ever will I sing. *Psalm 89* 1,2/6,7/15,16/17,18
Year A Proper 9 Closest to July 6 Hymn 376 or 331	**Zechariah 9:9–12** Lo, your king comes to you; triumphant and victorious is he, humble and riding on an ass.	**Psalm 145:8–14** *or* **Refrain:** I will exalt you, O God, my King, and bless your Name for ever and ever. *Psalm 145* 8,9/10,11/12,13

SECOND LESSON	CHANT BEFORE GOSPEL	GOSPEL
Romans 5:15b–19 If, because of one man's trespass, death reigned through that one man, much more will those who receive the abundance of grace and the free gift of righteousness reign in life through the one man Jesus Christ.	**Alleluia** *Ad libitum*	**Matthew 10:(16–23)24–33** Do not fear . . . you are of more value than many sparrows. Everyone who acknowledges me before men, I also will acknowledge before my Father who is in heaven.
Romans 6:3–11 All of us who have been baptized into Christ Jesus were baptized into his death.	**Alleluia** *Ad libitum*	**Matthew 10:34–42** Do not think that I have come to bring peace on earth. He who loves his father or mother . . . son or daughter more than me is not worthy of me.
Romans 7:21—8:6 I find it to be a law that when I want to do right, evil lies close at hand. Wretched man that I am! Who will deliver me from this body of death? Thanks be to God through Jesus Christ our Lord!	**Alleluia** *Ad libitum*	**Matthew 11:25–30** All things have been delivered to me by my Father. Come to me, all who labor. Take my yoke upon you, and learn from me, for I am gentle and lowly in heart, and you will find rest for your souls.

	FIRST LESSON	PSALM
Year A Proper 10 Closest to July 13 Hymn 401 or 195	**Isaiah 55:1–5,10–13** Ho, everyone who thirsts, come to the waters. As the rain and snow come down from heaven . . . so shall my word be . . . it shall accomplish that which I purpose.	**Psalm 65:9–14** *or* **Refrain:** Let the valleys shout for joy and sing. *Psalm 65* 9,10/11,12/13,14
Year A Proper 11 Closest to July 20 Hymn 523 or 446	**Wisdom 12:13,16–19** Thou who art sovereign in strength dost judge with mildness, and with great forbearance thou dost govern us; for thou hast power to act whenever thou dost choose.	**Psalm 86:11–17** *or* **Refrain:** You, O Lord, are good and forgiving. *Psalm 86* 11,12/13,14/16,17
Year A Proper 12 Closest to July 27 Hymn 280 or 298	**1 Kings 3:5–12** Solomon said, Give thy servant an understanding mind to govern thy people, that I may discern between good and evil. God said, Behold, I give you a wise and discerning mind.	**Psalm 119:129–136** *or* **Refrain:** When your word goes forth it gives light. *Psalm 119* 129,130/131,132/133, 134/135,136

SECOND LESSON	CHANT BEFORE GOSPEL	GOSPEL
Romans 8:9–17	**Alleluia**	**Matthew 13:1–9,18–23**
If the Spirit of him who raised Jesus from the dead dwells in you, he who raised Christ Jesus from the dead will give life to your mortal bodies.	*Ad libitum*	A sower went out to sow. He who hears the word and understands it; he indeed bears fruit.
Romans 8:18–25	**Alleluia**	**Matthew 13:24–30,36–43**
I consider that the sufferings of this present time are not worth comparing with the glory that is to be revealed to us.	*Ad libitum*	Let both grow together until the harvest; and at harvest time I will tell the reapers, Gather the weeds first and bind them in bundles to be burned, but gather the wheat into my barn.
Romans 8:26–34	**Alleluia**	**Matthew 13:31–33,44–49a**
The Spirit helps us in our weakness; for we do not know how to pray as we ought, but the Spirit himself intercedes for us.	*Ad libitum*	The kingdom of heaven is like a net which was thrown into the sea. When it was full, men drew it ashore and sat down and sorted the good into vessels but threw away the bad. So it will be at the close of the age.

FIRST LESSON   PSALM

Year A	**Nehemiah 9:16–20**	**Psalm 78:14–20,23–25**
Proper 13	Thou gavest thy good Spirit to instruct them, and didst not withhold thy manna from their mouth, and gavest them water for their thirst.	*or* **Refrain:** The Lord rained down manna from heaven. *Psalm 78* 14,15/17,18/19,23/24,25
Closest to August 3		
Hymn 213 or 192		

Year A	**Jonah 2:1–9**	**Psalm 29**
Proper 14	Jonah prayed to the Lord his God from the belly of the fish. The waters closed in over me. When my soul fainted within me, I remembered the Lord; and my prayer came to thee. Deliverance belongs to the Lord!	*or* **Refrain:** The Lord shall give strength to his people. *Psalm 29* 3,4/5,7/8,9/10,11
Closest to August 10		
Hymn 289		

Year A	**Isaiah 56:1(2–5)6–7**	**Psalm 67**
Proper 15	Foreigners who join themselves to the Lord . . . I will bring to my holy mountain. My house shall be called a house of prayer for all peoples.	*or* **Refrain:** Let the peoples praise you, O God; let all the peoples praise you. *Psalm 67* 1,2/4/6,7
Closest to August 17		
Hymn 263		

Year A	**Isaiah 51:1–6**	**Psalm 138**
Proper 16	Listen to me, my people . . . for a law will go forth from me, and my justice for a light to the peoples. My salvation will be for ever, and my deliverance will never be ended.	*or* **Refrain:** O Lord, your love endures for ever; do not abandon the work of your hands. *Psalm 138* 1,2/3,4/7,9
Closest to August 24		
Hymn 385		

SECOND LESSON	CHANT BEFORE GOSPEL	GOSPEL
Romans 8:35–39 I am sure that neither death, nor life . . . will be able to separate us from the love of God in Christ Jesus our Lord.	**Alleluia** *Ad libitum*	**Matthew 14:13–21** He blessed, and broke and gave the loaves to the disciples. Those who ate were about five thousand.
Romans 9:1–5 They are Israelites and to them belong the sonship, the glory, the promises. Of their race, according to the flesh, is the Christ.	**Alleluia** *Ad libitum*	**Matthew 14:22–23** Peter got out of the boat and walked on the water and came to Jesus; but when he saw the wind, he was afraid, and beginning to sink he cried out, Lord save me. Jesus immediately reached out his hand and caught him.
Romans 11:13–15,29–32 God has consigned all men to disobedience, that he may have mercy upon all.	**Alleluia** *Ad libitum*	**Matthew 15:21–28** A Canaanite woman from that region came out and cried, Have mercy on me, O Lord.
Romans 11:33–36 O the depth of the riches and . . . knowledge of God! How unsearchable are his judgments and how inscrutable his ways!	**Alleluia** *Ad libitum*	**Matthew 16:13–20** You are Peter, and on this rock I will build my church. I will give you the keys of the kingdom of heaven.

Year A	**Jeremiah 15:15–21**	**Psalm 26:1–8**
Proper 17	If you utter what is precious, and not what is worthless, you shall be as my mouth. They will fight against you, but they shall not prevail over you, for I am with you to save you and deliver you.	*or* **Refrain:** Your love, O Lord, is before my eyes. *Psalm 26* 1,2/4,5/6,7/8,12
Closest to August 31		
Hymn 337		

Year A	**Ezekiel 33:(1–6)7–11**	**Psalm 119:33–40**
Proper 18	You . . . I have made a watchman for the house of Israel. As I live, says the Lord God, I have no pleasure in the death of the wicked, but that the wicked turn from his way and live.	*or* **Refrain:** Make me go in the path of your commandments, for that is my desire. *Psalm 119* 33,34/35,36/37,38/39,40
Closest to Sept. 7		
Hymn 410		

Year A	**Ecclus. 27:30—28:7**	**Psalm 103:8–13**
Proper 19	Forgive your neighbor the wrong he has done, and then your sins will be pardoned.	*or* **Refrain:** The Lord is full of compassion and mercy, slow to anger and of great kindness. *Psalm 103* 1,2/9,10/11,12/13,14
Closest to Sept. 14		
Hymn 462		

Year A	**Jonah 3:10—4:11**	**Psalm 145:1–8**
Proper 20	When God saw what they did, how they turned from their evil way, God repented of the evil which he had said he would do to them.	*or* **Refrain:** The Lord is gracious and full of compassion. *Psalm 145* 1,2/3,4/5,6/7,8
Closest to Sept. 21		
Hymn 576		

SECOND LESSON	CHANT BEFORE GOSPEL	GOSPEL
Romans 12:1–8 As in one body we have many members, and all the members do not have the same function, so we . . . are one body in Christ . . . having gifts that differ.	**Alleluia** *Ad libitum*	**Matthew 16:21–27** If any man would come after me, let him deny himself and take up his cross and follow me.
Romans 12:9–21 Hate what is evil, hold fast to what is good. Do not be overcome by evil, but overcome evil with good.	**Alleluia** *Ad libitum*	**Matthew 18:15–20** If your brother sins against you, go and tell him his fault. Whatever you bind on earth will be bound in heaven, and whatever you loose on earth shall be loosed in heaven.
Romans 14:5–12 Why do you pass judgment on your brother? We shall all stand before the judgment seat of God.	**Alleluia** *Ad libitum*	**Matthew 18:21–35** How often shall my brother sin against me, and I forgive him? As many as seven times?
Phil. 1:21–27 Let your manner of life be worthy of the gospel of Christ.	**Alleluia** *Ad libitum*	**Matthew 20:1–16** The kingdom of heaven is like a householder who went out early in the morning to hire laborers. Am I not allowed to do what I choose with what belongs to me?

	FIRST LESSON	PSALM
Year A Proper 21 Closest to Sept. 28 Hymn 356	**Ezekiel 18:1-4,25-32** When a wicked man turns away from the wickedness he has committed . . . he shall save his life.	**Psalm 25:3-9** *or* **Refrain:** Remember, O Lord, your compassion and love, for they are from everlasting. *Psalm 25* 3,4/6,7/8,9
Year A Proper 22 Closest to Oct. 5 Hymn 519	**Isaiah 5:1-7** The vineyard of the Lord of hosts is the house of Israel. He looked for justice, but behold bloodshed; for righteousness, but behold, a cry!	**Psalm 80:7-14** *or* **Refrain** (Isaiah 5:7): The vineyard of the Lord of hosts is the house of Israel. *Psalm 80* 8,9/10,11/12,13/14,17
Year A Proper 23 Closest to Oct. 12 Hymn 442	**Isaiah 25:1-9** On this mountain, the Lord of hosts will make for all peoples a feast.	**Psalm 23** *or* **Refrain:** I will dwell in the house of the Lord for ever. *Psalm 23* 1,2/3,4/5,6
Year A Proper 24 Closest to Oct. 19 Hymn 542	**Isaiah 45:1-7** Thus says the Lord to his anointed, to Cyrus. I am the Lord, and there is no other, besides me there is no God.	**Psalm 96:1-9** *or* **Refrain:** Ascribe to the Lord honor and power. *Psalm 96* 1,2/3,4/5,6/8,9

SECOND LESSON	CHANT BEFORE GOSPEL	GOSPEL
Phil. 2:1–13	**Alleluia**	**Matthew 21:28–32**
Jesus did not count equality with God a thing to be grasped, but emptied himself, taking the form of a servant, being born in the likeness of men.	*Ad libitum*	Which of the two (sons) did the will of his father?
Phil. 3:14–21	**Alleluia**	**Matthew 21:33–43**
Our commonwealth is in heaven, and from it we await a Savior, the Lord Jesus Christ.	*Ad libitum*	This is the heir; come let us kill him and have his inheritance. The kingdom of God will be taken from you and given to a nation producing the fruits of it.
Phil. 4:4–13	**Alleluia**	**Matthew 22:1–14**
I can do all things in him who strengthens me.	*Ad libitum*	Friend, how did you get in here without a wedding garment? Many are called, but few are chosen.
1 Thess. 1:1–10	**Alleluia**	**Matthew 22:15–22**
Our gospel came to you not only in word, but also in power and in the Holy Spirit and with full conviction.	*Ad libitum*	Render . . . to Caesar the things that are Caesar's and to God the things that are God's.

	FIRST LESSON	PSALM
Year A	**Exodus 22:21–27**	**Psalm 1**
Proper 25	You shall not wrong a stranger or oppress	*or* **Refrain:** Happy are
Closest to Oct. 26	him, for you were strangers in the land of	they whose delight is in the law of the Lord.
Hymn 551 or 518	Egypt.	*Psalm 1* 1,2/3,4/5,6
Year A	**Micah 3:5–12**	**Psalm 43**
Proper 26	Thus says the Lord concerning the	*or* **Refrain:** Send out your
Closest to Nov. 2	prophets who lead my people astray, who cry	light and your truth, that they may lead me.
Hymn 501	"Peace" when they want something to eat, but declare war against him who puts nothing into their mouths . . . because of you Zion shall be plowed as a field.	*Psalm 43* 1,2/3,4/5,6
Year A	**Amos 5:18–24**	**Psalm 70**
Proper 27	Woe to you who desire the day of the Lord! It	*or* **Refrain:** O Lord, make
Closest to Nov. 9	is darkness and not light. Let justice roll	haste to help me.
Hymn 3	down like waters.	*Psalm 70* 1,2/3,4/5,6

SECOND LESSON	CHANT BEFORE GOSPEL	GOSPEL
1 Thess. 2:1–8 Just as we have been approved by God to be entrusted with the gospel, so we speak, not to please men, but to please God who tests our hearts.	**Alleluia** *Ad libitum*	**Matthew 22:34–46** Which is the great commandment in the law? You shall love the Lord . . . You shall love your neighbor.
1 Thess. 2:9–13,17–20 We worked night and day, that we might not burden any of you, while we preached to you the gospel of God.	**Alleluia** *Ad libitum*	**Matthew 23:1–12** The scribes and the Pharisees sit on Moses' seat; so practice and observe whatever they tell you, but not what they do; for they preach, but do not practice.
1 Thess. 4:13–18 The Lord himself will descend from heaven with a cry of command.	**Alleluia** (Matt. 24:42,44) Be watchful and ready,* for you know not when the Son of Man is coming.	**Matthew 25:1–13** The kingdom of heaven shall be compared to ten maidens who took their lamps and went to meet the bridgroom. Watch therefore, for you know neither the day nor the hour.

	FIRST LESSON	PSALM
Year A Proper 28 Closest to Nov. 16 Hymn 468 or 595	**Zeph. 1:7,12–18** The day of the Lord is at hand. I will bring distress on men. Neither their silver nor their gold shall be able to deliver them.	**Psalm 90:1–8,12** *or* **Refrain:** Teach us to number our days that we may apply our hearts to wisdom. *Psalm 90* 1,2/3,4/5,6/7,8
Year A Proper 29 Closest to Nov. 23 (Christ the King) Hymn 352 or 522	**Ezekiel 34:11–17** I myself will search for my sheep, and will seek them out. Behold, I judge between sheep and sheep, rams and he-goats.	**Psalm 95:1–7** *or* **Refrain:** We are the people of his pasture and the sheep of his hand. *Psalm 95* 1,2/3,4/5,6/7

1 Thess. 5:1–10	Alleluia	Matthew 25:14–15,19–29
You yourselves know well that the day of the Lord will come like a thief in the night. Let us keep awake and be sober . . . and put on the breastplate of faith.	(Rev. 2:10) Be faithful until death, says the Lord,* and I will give you the crown of life.	Well done, good and faithful servant; you have been faithful over a little, I will set you over much; enter into the joy of your master.

1 Cor. 15:20–28	Alleluia	Matthew 25:31–46
Then comes the end, when he delivers the kingdom to God the Father after destroying every rule and every authority and power.	(Mark 11:10) Blessed is the kingdom of our father David that is coming;* blessed is he who comes in the name of the Lord.	When the Son of man comes in his glory . . . he will sit on his glorious throne. Before him will be gathered all the nations, and he will separate them one from another as a shepherd separates the sheep from the goats.

Year B

The themes of the Advent Sundays are the same in all three years.

SEE PAGES 202–205 FOR
OTHER SUGGESTED
HYMNS

	FIRST LESSON	PSALM
Year B 1 Advent (The final Advent) Hymn 3	**Isaiah 64:1–9a** O that thou wouldst rend the heavens and come down. No one has heard . . . no eye has seen a God besides thee, who works for those who wait for him.	**Psalm 80:1–7** *or* **Refrain:** Restore us, O God of hosts; show the light of your countenance, and we shall be saved. *Psalm 80* 1,2/4,14/16,17
Year B 2 Advent (The Ministry of John the Baptist) Hymn 10	**Isaiah 40:1–11** Comfort, comfort my people, says your God. A voice cries: In the wilderness prepare the way of the Lord.	**Psalm 85:7–13** *or* **Refrain:** Show us your mercy, O Lord, and grant us your salvation. *Psalm 85* 8,9/10,11/12,13
Year B 3 Advent (The Ministry of John the Baptist)	**Isaiah 65:17–25** Behold, I create new heavens and a new earth; and the former things shall not be remembered.	**Canticle 3 or 15** *or* **Psalm 126** *or* **Refrain:** My soul proclaims the greatness of the Lord. *Canticle 15* 1,2/3,4/5,6/7,8 *or* **Refrain:** The Lord has done great things for us, and we are glad indeed. *Psalm 126* 1,2/3,4/5,6/7

SECOND LESSON	ALLELUIA	GOSPEL
1 Cor. 1:1–9	**Alleluia**	**Mark 13:(24–32)33–37**
Wait for the revealing of our Lord Jesus Christ; who will sustain you to the end, guiltless in the day of our lord.	(Psalm 85:7) Show us your mercy, O Lord,* and grant us your salvation.	Watch therefore—for you do not know when the master of the house will come.
2 Peter 3:8–15a,18	**Alleluia**	**Mark 1:1–8**
According to his promise we wait for new heavens and a new earth in which righteousness dwells.	(Luke 3:4,6) Prepare the way of the Lord, make his paths straight;* and all flesh shall see the salvation of our God.	John the baptizer appeared in the wilderness, preaching a baptism of repentance for the forgiveness of sins.
1 Thessalonians 5:(12–15)16–28	**Alleluia**	**John 1:6–8,19–28**
Rejoice always . . . may your spirit and soul and body be kept sound and blameless at the coming of our Lord Jesus Christ.	(Luke 4:18) The Spirit of the Lord is upon me;* he has anointed me to preach good tidings to the poor.	This is the testimony of John. Among you stands one whom you do not know, even he who comes after me.
		or **John 3:23–30** I said, I am not the Christ, but I have been sent before him.

Year B	**2 Samuel 7:4,8–16**	**Psalm 132:8–15**
4 Advent	I will make for you a great name. Your house and your kingdom shall be made sure for ever before me; and your throne shall be established for ever.	*or* **Refrain:** Arise, O Lord, into your resting-place, you and the ark of your strength. *Psalm 132* 9,10/11,12/14,15
(The Annunciation)		
Hymn 2 or 317 (1,2)		

Year ABC	**Isaiah 9:2–4,6–7**	**Psalm 96:1–4,11–12**
Christmas Day I	The people who walked in darkness have seen a great light. For to us a child is born . . . and the government will be upon his shoulder.	*or* **Refrain** (Luke 2:11): Today is born our Savior, Christ the Lord. *Psalm 96* 1,2/3,4/11,12
(At Midnight)		
Hymn 20 or 42		

Year ABC	**Isaiah 62:6–7,10–12**	**Psalm 97:1–4,11–12**
Christmas Day II	Say to the daughter of Zion, Behold, your salvation comes. They shall be called the holy people, the redeemed of the Lord.	*or* **Refrain** (Isa. 9:6): To us a child is born; to us a Son is given. *Psalm 97* 1,2/3,4/11,12
(At Dawn)		
Hymn 13		

Year ABC	**Isaiah 52:7–10**	**Psalm 98:1–6**
Christmas Day III	How beautiful upon the mountains are the feet of him who brings good tidings. All the ends of the earth shall see the salvation of our God.	*or* **Refrain:** All the ends of the earth have seen the salvation of our God. *Psalm 98* 1,2/3,4/5,6
(During the Day)		
Hymn 18		

SECOND LESSON	ALLELUIA	GOSPEL
Romans 16:25–27	**Alleluia**	**Luke 1:26–38**
The revelation of the mystery . . . now disclosed . . . is made known to all nations, according to the command of the eternal God, to bring about the obedience of faith.	(Luke 1:38) Behold, I am the handmaid of the Lord;* let it be to me according to your word.	Hail, O favored one, the Lord is with you! You will conceive. The Lord God will give to him the throne of his father David. Behold, I am the handmaid of the Lord; let it be to me according to your word.
Titus 2:11–14	**Alleluia**	**Luke 2:1–14(15–20)**
The grace of God has appeared for the salvation of all . . . the appearing of the glory of our great God and Savior Jesus Christ.	(Luke 2:10,11) Behold, I bring you good tidings of great joy;* to you is born a Savior, Christ the Lord.	To you is born this day in the city of David a Savior, who is Christ the Lord.
Titus 3:4–7	**Alleluia**	**Luke 2:(1–14)15–20**
He saved us . . . by the washing of regeneration and renewal in the Holy Spirit.	(Luke 2:14) Glory to God in the highest,* and peace to his people on earth.	Let us go over to Bethlehem and see this thing that has happened, which the Lord has made known to us.
Hebrews 1:1–12	**Alleluia**	**John 1:1–14**
God spoke of old . . . by the prophets; but in these last days he has spoken to us by a Son . . . through whom also he created the world. Thou art my Son, today I have begotten thee.	(John 1:14) The Word was made flesh and dwelt among us,* full of grace and truth.	The Word became flesh and dwelt among us, full of grace and truth.

Year ABC	**Isaiah 61:10—62:3**	**Psalm 147:13-21**
First Sunday after Christmas	The Lord God will cause righteousness and praise to spring forth before all the nations.	*or* **Refrain** (John 1:14): The Word was made flesh and dwelt among us. *Psalm 147* 13,14/15,16/20,21
(The Incarnation)		
Hymn 17		

Year ABC	**Exodus 34:1-8**	**Psalm 8**
The Holy Name of our Lord Jesus Christ	Moses cut two tables of stone . . . and went up on Mount Sinai. The Lord descended in the cloud and stood with him there and proclaimed the name of the Lord.	*or* **Refrain:** O Lord our Governor, how exalted is your Name in all the world. *Psalm 8* 4,5/6,7/8,9
January 1		
Hymn 326		

Year ABC	**Jeremiah 31:7-14**	**Psalm 84:1-8**
Second Sunday after Christmas	Behold, I will bring them from the north country . . . the woman with child and her who is in travail together; a great company, they shall return here. I am a father to Israel, and Ephraim is my first-born.	*or* **Refrain:** How dear to me is your dwelling, O Lord of hosts. *Psalm 84* 1bc,2/3,4/5,6/7,8
(The Holy Family)		
Hymn 504 or 35		

SECOND LESSON	ALLELUIA	GOSPEL
Gal. 3:23–25; 4:4–7 God sent forth his Son, born of a woman, born under the law, to redeem those who were under the law, so that we might receive adoption as sons.	**Alleluia** (John 1:14) We have seen his glory;* glory that is his as the Father's only Son.	**John 1:1–18** To all who received him he gave power to become the children of God. The law was given through Moses; grace and truth came through Jesus Christ.
Romans 1:1–7 The Gospel of God which he promised beforehand through his prophets in the holy scriptures, the gospel concerning his Son, who was descended from David according to the flesh.	**Alleluia** (Heb. 1:1,2) In the past God spoke to our fathers through the prophets,* but now he has spoken to us through his Son.	**Luke 2:15–21** At the end of eight days, when he was circumcised, he was called Jesus, the name given by the angel before he was conceived in the womb.
Eph. 1:3–6,15–19a Blessed be the God and Father of our Lord Jesus Christ. He destined us in love to be his sons through Jesus Christ.	**Alleluia** (John 1:14) The Word was made flesh and dwelt among us,* full of grace and truth.	**Matt. 2:13–15,19–23** Take the child and his mother. "Out of Egypt have I called my son." *or* **Luke 2:41–52** After three days they found him in the temple. *or* **Matt. 2:1–12** Wise men from the east came to Jerusalem, saying, Where is he who has been born king of the Jews?

	FIRST LESSON	PSALM
Year ABC The Epiphany January 6 Hymn 47	Isaiah 60:1-6,9 Nations shall come to your light, and kings to the brightness of your rising. They shall bring gold and frankincense.	Psalm 72:1-2,10-17 *or* **Refrain:** All kings shall bow down before him; all the nations shall do him service. *Psalm 72* 1,2/8,10/12,13/17
Year B 1 Epiphany (The Baptism of Our Lord) Hymn 545 Entrance Hymn 53	Isaiah 42:1-9 Behold my servant, whom I uphold, my chosen, in whom my soul delights; I have put my Spirit upon him.	Psalm 89:20-29 *or* **Refrain:** I have found David my servant; with my holy oil have I anointed him. *Psalm 89* 21,22/24,25/26,27/28,29
Year B 2 Epiphany Hymn 575 or 563	1 Sam. 3:1-10(11-20) The Lord called, Samuel. And Samuel said, Speak, for thy servant hears.	Psalm 63:1-8 *or* **Refrain:** O God, you are my God; eagerly I seek you. *Psalm 63* 1bc,2/3,4/5,6/7,8

Eph. 3:1–12

Grace was given to
preach to the Gentiles
the unsearchable riches
of Christ.

Alleluia

(Matt. 2:2)
We have seen his star in
the east,* and have
come to worship the
Lord.

Matthew 2:1–12

Wise men from the east
came to Jerusalem,
saying, Where is he
who has been born king
of the Jews? They
offered him gifts, gold
and frankincense and
myrrh.

Acts 10:34–38

Good news of peace by
Jesus Christ . . .
beginning from Galilee
after the baptism which
John preached: How
God anointed Jesus of
Nazareth with the Holy
Spirit.

Alleluia

(Gal. 3:27)
All of you who were
baptized into Christ*
have clothed yourselves
with Christ.

Mark 1:7–11

When Jesus came up
out of the water,
immediately he saw the
heavens opened and
the Spirit descending.
Thou art my beloved
Son.

1 Cor. 6:11b–20

The body is not meant
for immorality but for
the Lord, and the Lord
for the body. Your
bodies are members of
Christ.

Alleluia

(1 Sam. 3:9; John 6:68)
Speak, O Lord, your
servant is listening:*
you have the words of
everlasting life.

John 1:43–51

Jesus found Philip and
said to him, Follow me.
Philip found
Nathanael.

*The Gospel Lessons for the remaining Sundays after Epiphany present
the beginnings of our Lord's ministry. During Year B they are chosen
from the Gospel according to Mark. The Old Testament lessons are
selected to match the Gospels. The Epistles consist of a semi-
continuous reading of the Corinthian Epistles which were introduced
last Sunday.*

SEE PAGES 202–205 FOR
OTHER SUGGESTED
HYMNS

	FIRST LESSON	PSALM
Year B 3 Epiphany Hymn 566 or 437 (tune 391)	**Jeremiah 3:21—4:2** Return, O faithless sons, I will heal your faithlessness. Behold, we come to thee; for thou art the Lord our God.	**Psalm 130** *or* **Refrain:** With the Lord there is mercy; with him there is plenteous redemption. *Psalm 130* 1/2,3/4,5/6,7
Year B 4 Epiphany Hymn 417 or 272	**Deuteronomy 18:15–20** I will raise up for them a prophet like you from among the brethren; and I will put my words in his mouth, and he shall speak to them all that I command.	**Psalm 111** *or* **Refrain:** The fear of the Lord is the beginning of wisdom. *Psalm 111* 1,2/7,8/9,10
Year B 5 Epiphany Hymn 282	**2 Kings 4:(8–17)18–21(22–31) 32–37** When Elisha came into the house, he saw the child lying dead on the bed. He prayed . . . and as he stretched himself upon him, the flesh became warm. The child opened his eyes.	**Psalm 142** *or* **Refrain:** You are my refuge, O Lord; my portion in the land of the living. *Psalm 142* 1,2/3,4/6,7

SECOND LESSON	ALLELUIA	GOSPEL
1 Cor. 7:17–23	**Alleluia**	**Mark 1:14–20**
Let every one lead the life which the Lord has assigned to him, and in which God has called him.	(Mark 1:15) The kingdom of God is near;* repent and believe the Gospel.	Repent, and believe in the Gospel. I will make you fishers of men.
1 Cor. 8:1b–13	**Alleluia**	**Mark 1:21–28**
"Knowledge" puffs up, but love builds up. If anyone imagines that he knows something, he does not yet know as he ought to know. But if one loves God, one is known by him.	*Ad libitum* *(See page 206)*	Jesus went into the synagogue and taught. They were astonished at his teaching, for he taught them as one who had authority, and not as the scribes.
1 Cor. 9:16–23	**Alleluia**	**Mark 1:29–39**
If I preach the gospel, that gives me no ground for boasting. For necessity is laid upon me. Woe to me if I do not preach the gospel. I have become all things to all men, that I might by all means save some.	*Ad libitum*	Simon's mother-in-law lay sick with a fever. Jesus came and took her by the hand and lifted her up, and the fever left her; and she served them.

	FIRST LESSON	PSALM
Year B 6 Epiphany Hymn 517 or 424	**2 Kings 5:1–15ab** Elisha sent a messenger to Naaman the Syrian saying, Go and wash in the Jordan seven times.	**Psalm 42:1–7** *or* **Refrain:** As the deer longs for the water-brooks, so longs my soul for you, O God. *Psalm 42* *2,3/4,5/6,7*
Year B 7 Epiphany Hymn 567	**Isaiah 43:18–25** Behold, I am doing a new thing. I am He who blots out your transgressions . . . and I will not remember your sins.	**Psalm 32:1–8** *or* **Refrain:** Happy are they whose transgressions are forgiven, and whose sin is put away. *Psalm 32* *3,4/5,6/7,8*
Year B 8 Epiphany Hymn 479	**Hosea 2:14–23** In that day, says the Lord, you will call me "My husband." I will betroth you to me for ever.	**Psalm 103:1–6** *or* **Refrain:** The Lord is full of compassion and mercy, slow to anger and of great kindness. *Psalm 103* *1,2/3,4/5,6*
Year B Last Sunday After Epiphany (The Transfiguration) Hymn 119 Dismissal Hymn 54	**1 Kings 19:9–18** Elijah came to a cave and dwelt there. After the earthquake a fire, but the Lord was not in the fire; and after the fire a still small voice.	**Psalm 27:5–11** *or* **Refrain:** The Lord is my light and my salvation. *Psalm 27* *5,6/7,9/10,11*

SECOND LESSON	ALLELUIA	GOSPEL
1 Cor. 9:24–27	**Alleluia**	**Mark 1:40–45**
Do you not know that in a race all the runners compete, but only one receives the prize? So run that you may obtain it.	*Ad libitum*	A leper came to Jesus. Moved with pity he stretched out his hand and touched him. The leprosy left him.
2 Cor. 1:18–22	**Alleluia**	**Mark 2:1–12**
All the promises of God find their Yes in him (Jesus).	*Ad libitum*	The Son of man has authority on earth to forgive sins. Rise . . . walk.
2 Cor. 3:(4–11)17—4:2	**Alleluia**	**Mark 2:18–22**
Now the Lord is the Spirit, and where the Spirit of the Lord is, there is freedom.	*Ad libitum*	Can the wedding guests fast while the bridegroom is with them? The days will come, when the bridegroom is taken away from them, and then they will fast in that day.
2 Peter 1:16–19(20–21)	**Alleluia** (Matt. 17:5) This is my Son, my Beloved,* with whom I am well pleased.	**Mark 9:2–9**
We were eyewitnesses of his majesty. For when he received honor and glory from God . . . we were with him on the holy mountain.		There appeared to them Elijah with Moses . . . talking to Jesus. This is my beloved Son; listen to him.

Year ABC	**Joel 2:1–2,12–17**	**Psalm 103:8–14**
Ash Wednesday	Return to me with all your heart, with fasting, with weeping. Return to the Lord, your God, for he is gracious and merciful.	*or* **Refrain:** The Lord remembers that we are but dust. *Psalm 103* 8,9/10,11/12,13
Hymn 56 Dismissal Hymn 61		

or **Isaiah 58:1–12**
Cry aloud . . . declare
to my people their
transgression. Is not
this the fast I choose: to
loose the bonds of
wickedness . . . to let
the oppressed go free?

Proper Liturgy, page 264

The Lessons appointed for the Season of Lent are intended as background and preparation for Easter. The Old Testament Lessons present a synopsis of the history of salvation from the Story of the Flood to the return from Babylon. The Gospels, beginning with the Third Sunday, consist of a series of readings from John's Gospel. The Epistles frequently match the Old Testament Lessons.

Year B	**Genesis 9:8–17**	**Psalm 25:3–9**
1 Lent	*The Covenant with Noah*	*or* **Refrain:** Your paths, O Lord, are love and faithfulness, to those who keep your covenant. *Psalm 25* 3,4/5,6/7,8
(The Temptation of our Lord)	This is the sign of the covenant which I make between me and you and every living creature . . . I set my bow in the cloud.	
Hymn 61		

[76]

SECOND LESSON	CHANT BEFORE GOSPEL	GOSPEL
2 Cor. 5:20b—6:10	**Verse***	**Matt. 6:1–6,16–21**
Behold, now is the acceptable time; behold, now is the day of salvation.	(2 Cor. 6:2) Behold, now is the acceptable time;* behold, now is the day of salvation.	Beware of practicing your piety before men in order to be seen by them; for then you will have no reward from your Father who is in heaven.
	or **Tract** Psalm 130:1–4(5–7)	
	* *See the Introduction*	

1 Peter 3:18–22	**Verse**	**Mark 1:9–13**
God's patience waited in the days of Noah, during the building of the ark, in which . . . eight persons were saved through water.	(Matt. 4:4) Man shall not live by bread alone,* but by every word that proceeds from the mouth of God.	Jesus came from Nazareth . . . and was baptized. Thou art my beloved Son. He was in the wilderness forty days tempted by Satan.
	or **Tract** Psalm 91:1–4,9–11	

	FIRST LESSON	PSALM
Year B	**Genesis 22:1–14**	**Psalm 16:5–11**
2 Lent	*The Sacrifice of Isaac*	*or*
Hymn 522 or 417	God tested Abraham. Now I know that you fear God, seeing you have not withheld your son, your only son.	**Refrain:** The Lord will show me the path of life. *Psalm 16* 5,6/7,8/9,10/11
Year B	**Exodus 20:1–17**	**Psalm 19:7–14**
3 Lent	*The Ten Commandments*	*or*
Hymn 497	I am the Lord your God, who brought you out of the land of Egypt, out of the house of bondage. You shall have no other gods before me.	**Refrain**(John 6:68): Lord, you have the words of everlasting life. *Psalm 19* 7,8/9,10/11,12/13,14
Year B	**2 Chron. 36:14–23**	**Psalm 122**
4 Lent	*The Restoration of Jerusalem*	*or*
(The Communion Banquet)	Thus says Cyrus king of Persia, The Lord, the God of heaven, has given me all the kingdoms of the earth, and he has charged me to build him a house at Jerusalem.	**Refrain:** I was glad when they said to me, Let us go to the house of the Lord. *Psalm 122* 2,3,4/5,6,7/8,9
Hymn 195 Entrance Hymn 597 Dismissal Hymn 585		

SECOND LESSON	CHANT BEFORE GOSPEL	GOSPEL
Romans 8:31–39	**Verse**	**Mark 8:31–38**
If God is for us, who is against us? He who did not spare his own Son but gave him up for us all, will he not also give us all things with him?	(Mark 8:34) If anyone would come after me,* let him take up his cross and follow me. *or* **Tract** Psalm 106:1–5 (*Omit the initial Hallelujah*)	The Son of man must suffer many things . . . and be killed, and after three days rise again. Whoever would save his life will lose it; and whoever loses his life for my sake and the gospel's will save it.
Romans 7:13–25	**Verse**	**John 2:13–22**
We know that the law is spiritual; but I am carnal, sold under sin. I delight in the law of God, in my inmost self, but I see in my members another law at war with the law of my mind.	(Amos 5:14) Seek good, and not evil, that you may live;* and the God of hosts will be with you. *or* **Tract** Psalm 42:1–7	Jesus went up to Jerusalem. In the temple he found those who were selling oxen and sheep. Take these things away, you shall not make my Father's house a house of trade.
Eph. 2:4–10	**Verse**	**John 6:4–15**
By grace you have been saved through faith; and this is not your own doing, it is the gift of God.	(John 6:51) I am the living bread which came down from heaven;* if anyone eats of this bread, he will live for ever. *or* **Tract** Psalm 125	Jesus took the loaves, and when he had given thanks, he distributed them to those who were seated.

Year B	**Jeremiah 31:31–34**	**Psalm 51:11–16**
5 Lent	*Prophecy of a New Covenant*	*or*
Hymn 71	I will put my law within them, and I will write it upon their hearts; and I will be their God and they shall be my people.	**Refrain:** Create in me a clean heart, O God. *Psalm 51* 1,2/11,12/13,14/15,16

Year B	**Isaiah 45:21–25**	**Psalm 22:1–11**
The Sunday of The Passion	Turn to me and be saved. To me every knee shall bow.	*or*
or	*or* **Isaiah 52:13—53:12**	**Refrain:** My God, my God, why have you forsaken me?
Palm Sunday	He has borne our griefs. He was wounded for our transgressions.	*Psalm 22* 1,2,3/4,5,6/7,8,9/10,11
Hymn 68 or 67 Dismissal Hymn 75		

Liturgy of the Palms: Page 270. Gospel of the Palms: Mark 11:1–11a. At the Procession: Hymn 62 & Psalm 118:19–29. Refrain after each verse of the Psalm: Hosanna in the highest.

SECOND LESSON	CHANT BEFORE GOSPEL	GOSPEL
Hebrews 5:(1–4)5–10	**Verse**	**John 12:20–33**
Christ did not exalt himself to be made a high priest, but was appointed. He learned obedience through what he suffered.	(John 12:26) If any one serves me, he must follow me, says the Lord;* and where I am, there shall my servant also be.	The hour has come for the Son of man to be glorified. I, when I am lifted up from earth, will draw all men to myself.
	or **Tract** Psalm 129:1–4(5–8)	

Philippians 2:5–11	**Verse**	**Mark 14:32—15:39(40–47)**
He humbled himself and became obedient unto death . . . that at the name of Jesus every knee should bow.	(Phil. 2:8,9) Christ for us became obedient unto death, even death on a cross;* therefore God has highly exalted him and bestowed on him the name which is above every name.	*or* **Mark 15:1–39(40–47)** *The Passion of our Lord Jesus Christ.*
	or **Tract** Psalm 22:26–30.	

	FIRST LESSON	PSALM
Year ABC Monday in Holy Week Hymn 69	Isaiah 42:1–9 *First Song of the Servant of Yahweh* Behold my servant, whom I uphold, my chosen, in whom my soul delights: I have put my Spirit upon him, he will bring forth justice to the nations.	Psalm 36:5–10 *or* **Refrain:** In your light, O God, we see light. *Psalm 36* 5,6/7,8/9,10
Year ABC Tuesday in Holy Week Hymn 73	Isaiah 49:1–6 *Second Song of the Servant of Yahweh* It is too light a thing that you should be my servant to raise up the tribes of Jacob and to restore the preserved of Israel; I will give you as a light to the nations, that my salvation may reach to the end of the earth.	Psalm 71:1–12 *or* **Refrain:** I have taken refuge in you, O Lord. *Psalm 71* 2,3/4,10/11,12

Hebrews 11:39—12:3

Looking to Jesus . . .
who for the joy that was
set before him endured
the cross, despising the
shame, and is seated at
the right hand of the
throne of God.

Verse

We adore you, O
Christ, and we bless
you,* because by your
holy cross you have
redeemed the world.

or **Tract**
Psalm 102:1–4, 12–13

John 12:1–11

Six days before the
Passover, Jesus came to
Bethany. Mary took a
pound of costly
ointment . . . and
anointed the feet of
Jesus.

or **Mark 14:3–9**

She has anointed my
body beforehand for
burying. And truly, I
say to you . . . what
she has done will be
told in memory of her.

---

1 Cor. 1:18–31

The word of the cross is
folly to those who are
perishing, but to us who
are being saved it is the
power of God.

Verse or Tract

As on Monday

John 12:37–38, 42–50

Jesus said, He who
believes in me, believes
not in me but in him
who sent me.

or **Mark 11:15–19**
Jesus entered the
temple and began to
drive out those who
sold and those who
bought. Is it not
written, "My house
shall be called a house
of prayer for all the
nations?"

	FIRST LESSON	PSALM
Year ABC	**Isaiah 50:4–9a**	**Psalm 69:7–15,22–23**
Wednesday in Holy Week	*Third Song of the Servant of Yahweh*	*or* **Refrain:** Answer me, O God, in your great mercy. *Psalm 69* 7,8/9,10/14,15/22,23
Hymn 81	I gave my back to the smiters, and my cheeks to those who pulled out the beard; I hid not my face from shame and spitting.	

Year ABC	**Exodus 12:1–14a**	**Psalm 78:14–20,23–25**
Maundy Thursday	This month shall be for you the beginning of months. They shall take every man a lamb . . . a lamb for a household. It is the Lord's passover.	*or* **Refrain:** Mortals ate the bread of angels, for the Lord gave them manna from heaven. *Psalm 78* 14,15/17,18/19,23/24,25
(The Lord's Supper)		
Hymn 195		
Proper Liturgy, page 274		

Year ABC	**Isaiah 52:13—53:12**	**Psalm 22:1–11**
Good Friday	He was wounded for our transgressions . . . He was numbered with the transgressors.	*or* **Refrain:** My God, my God, why have you forsaken me? *Psalm 22* 1,2/7,8/14,15/16,17/18, 19/20,21
Hymn 75		
	or **Genesis 22:1–18** You have not withheld your son, your only son.	
	or **Wisdom 2:1,12–24** If the righteous man is God's son, he will help him. Let us condemn him to a shameful death.	
Proper Liturgy, page 276		

SECOND LESSON	CHANT BEFORE GOSPEL	GOSPEL
Heb. 9:11–15,24–28 When Christ appeared as a high priest of the good things that have come . . . he entered once for all into the Holy Place, taking . . . his own blood, thus securing an eternal redemption.	**Verse or Tract** *As on Monday*	**John 13:21–35** Jesus testified, Truly, truly, I say to you, one of you will betray me. *or* **Matt. 26:1–5,14–25** Judas went to the chief priests and said, What will you give me if I deliver him to you?
1 Corinthians 11:23–26(27–32) This is my body. This cup is the new covenant in my blood. Do this in remembrance of me.	**Verse** (John 13:34) A new commandment I give to you:* love one another as I have loved you. *or* **Tract** Psalm 43	**John 13:1–15** Jesus began to wash the disciples' feet. *or* **Luke 22:14–30** Jesus took a cup, and . . . said, Take this, and divide it. He took bread, and broke it, saying, This is my body.

Hymns 199 and 200 may appropriately be sung after the postcommunion prayer.

Hebrews 10:1–25 "A body hast thou prepared for me." By a single offering he has perfected for all time those who are sanctified. There is no longer any offering for sin.	**Verse** (Phil. 2:8,9) Christ for us became obedient unto death, even death on a cross;* therefore God has highly exalted him and bestowed on him the name which is above every name. *or* **Tract** Psalm 40:1–14 *or* Psalm 69:1–10,14–23	**John (18:1–40); 19:1–37** *The Passion of our Lord Jesus Christ.* It is finished.

HYMNS	FIRST LESSON	PSALM

Year ABC	**Job 14:1–14**	**Psalm 31:1–5**
Holy Saturday	If a man die, shall he	*or*
	live again?	**Refrain** (Luke 23:46):
Hymn 83		Father, into your hands
		I commend my spirit.
		Psalm 31
		1,2/3,4/5,16

Proper Liturgy, page 283

SECOND LESSON	CHANT BEFORE GOSPEL	GOSPEL
1 Peter 4:1–8	**Verse**	**Matthew 27:57–66**
The Gentiles will give account to him who is ready to judge the living and the dead. This is why the gospel was preached even to the dead.	We adore you, O Christ, and we bless you,* because by your holy cross you have redeemed the world. *or* **Tract** Psalm 130	*or* **John 19:38–42** *The Burial of our Lord Jesus Christ.*

The Great Vigil of Easter: Liturgy of the Word.

At least two of the following Lessons are read, of which one is always the Lesson from Exodus. Four or five Lessons are customary. After each Lesson, the Psalm or Canticle listed, or some other suitable psalm, canticle, or hymn may be sung. A period of silence may be kept, and the Collect provided, or some other suitable Collect may be said. The entire Great Vigil of Easter may be found on pages 284–285 of the Prayer Book.

1. **Genesis 1:1—2:2**

   The Story of Creation

   Psalm 33:1–11
   or Psalm 36:5–10

   or
   Refrain: By the word of the Lord were the heavens made, by the breath of his mouth all the heavenly hosts.
   Psalm 33
   1,2/3,4/5,7/8,9/10,11

   or
   Refrain: In your light, O God, we see light.
   Psalm 36
   5,6/7,8/9,10

2. **Genesis 7:1–5,11–18; 8:6–18; 9:8–13**

   The Flood

   Psalm 46

   or
   Refrain: The Lord of hosts is with us; the God of Jacob is our stronghold.
   Psalm 46
   1,2,3/5,6,7/9,10,11

3. **Genesis 22:1–18**

   Abraham's sacrifice of Isaac

   Psalm 33:12–22
   or Psalm 16

   or
   Refrain: Happy is the nation whose God is the Lord.
   Psalm 33
   13,14,15/16,18,19/20,21,22

   or
   Refrain: Protect me, O God, for I take refuge in you.
   Psalm 16
   5,6/8,9/10,11

4. **Exodus 14:10—15:1**

   Israel's deliverance at the Red Sea

   Canticle 8, The Song of Moses

   or
   Refrain: I will sing to the Lord, for he has risen up in might.
   Canticle 8
   1,2/3,4/5,6/7,8/9,10/11,12,13

5. Isaiah 4:2–6

*God's Presence in a
Renewed Israel*

6. Isaiah 55:1–11

*Salvation offered freely to
all*

7. Ezekiel 36:24–28

*A new heart and a new
spirit.*

8. Ezekiel 37:1–14

The valley of dry bones

9. Zephaniah 3:12–20

*The gathering of God's
people*

Psalm 122

or
Refrain: Pray for the peace of Jerusalem.
Psalm 122
1,2/3,4/6,7/8,9
Canticle 9, The First Song of Isaiah

or
Refrain: You shall draw water with rejoicing
from the springs of salvation.
Canticle 9
1,2/4,5/6,7
Psalm 42:1–7

or
Refrain: As the deer longs for the water-brooks,
so longs my soul for you, O God.
Psalm 42
2,3/4,5/6,7
Psalm 30
or **Psalm 143**

or
Refrain: You brought me up, O Lord, from the
dead.
Psalm 30
1,2,3/4,5,6/12,13

or
Refrain: Revive me, O Lord for your Name's
sake.
Psalm 143
1,2/4,5/6,7/8,10
Psalm 98
or **Psalm 126**

or
Refrain: Shout with joy to the Lord, all you
lands; lift up your voice, rejoice, and sing.
Psalm 98
1,2/3,4/6,7/8,9

or
Refrain: The Lord has done great things for us,
and we are glad indeed.
Psalm 126
1,2/3,4/5,6/7

Year ABC	*After the Collect of the Vigil Eucharist, continue with the Epistle.*	
Easter Day		
At the Vigil or Early Service	*At an early Service, use one of the Old Testament Lessons from the Vigil followed by the corresponding Psalm or Canticle.*	

Year B	**Acts 10:34–43**	**Psalm 118:14–17,22–24**
Easter Day	God raised him on the third day and made him manifest.	*or*
Principal Service		**Refrain:** On this day the Lord has acted; we will rejoice and be glad in it.
Hymn 97	*or* **Isaiah 25:6–9** He will swallow up death for ever.	*Psalm 118* 14,15/16,17/22,23

Year ABC	**Acts 5:29a,30–32**	**Psalm 114** *or* **Psalm 118:14–17,22–24** *or* **Psalm 136**
Easter Day	The God of our fathers raised Jesus whom you killed by hanging him on a tree.	
Evening Service		*or* **Refrain:** Hallelujah!
Hymn 207	*or* **Daniel 12:1–3** Many of those who sleep in the dust of the earth shall awake, some to everlasting life, and some to shame and everlasting contempt.	*Psalm 114* 1,2/3,4/5,6/7,8 *or Psalm 118 as at the principal service*

Romans 6:3–11	**Alleluia**	**Matthew 28:1–10**
All of us who have been baptized into Christ Jesus were baptized into his death . . . so that as Christ was raised . . . we too might walk in newness of life.	V. Alleluia. R. Alleluia. *Repeated three times, followed by:* **Refrain:** Hallelujah! *Psalm 114* 1,2/3,4/5,6/7,8 *If preferred, the Psalm may be sung without Refrain.*	After the sabbath, toward the dawn of the first day of the week . . . He is not here; for he has risen. *Offertory Hymn:*89
Colossians 3:1–4	**Alleluia**	**Mark 16:1–8**
You have been raised with Christ. For you have died, and your life is hid with Christ in God. *or* Acts 10:34–43	(1 Cor. 5:7,8) Christ our Passover is sacrificed for us:* therefore let us keep the feast.	Very early on the first day of the week, they went to the tomb.
1 Cor. 5:6b–8	**Alleluia**	**Luke 24:13–35**
Christ, our paschal lamb, has been sacrificed. Let us, therefore, celebrate the festival, not with the old leaven, the leaven of malice and evil, but with the unleavened bread of sincerity and truth. *or* Acts 5:29a,30–32	*As at the Morning Service*	That very day two of them were going to a village named Emmaus . . . When he was at table with them, he took the bread and blessed, and broke it, and gave it to them. And their eyes were opened and they recognized him.

	FIRST LESSON	PSALM
Year ABC Monday in Easter Week Hymn 91	**Acts 2:14,22b–32** Peter addressed them. This Jesus, delivered up according to the definite plan and foreknowledge of God, you crucified and killed by the hands of lawless men. But God raised him up. Of that we all are witnesses.	**Psalm 16:8–11** *or* **Psalm 118:19–24** *or* **Refrain:** Hallelujah! *Psalm 16* 8/9/10/11 *or* **Refrain:** Give thanks to the Lord, for he is good; his mercy endures for ever. *or* Hallelujah! *Psalm 118* 19,20/21,22/23,24
Year ABC Tuesday in Easter Week Hymn 100 (tune 113)	**Acts 2:36–41** Let all the house of Israel therefore know assuredly that God has made him both Lord and Christ. Repent, and be baptized.	**Psalm 33:18–22** *or* **Refrain:** Hallelujah! *Psalm 33* 1,2/18,19/20,21 *or Psalm 118 as on Monday*
Year ABC Wednesday in Easter Week Hymn 207	**Acts 3:1–10** Peter said, I have no silver and gold, but I give you what I have; in the name of Jesus Christ of Nazareth, walk.	**Psalm 105:1–8** *or* **Refrain:** Hallelujah! *Psalm 105* 1,2/3,4/5,6/7,8 *or Psalm 118 as on Monday*

	Alleluia	Matthew 28:9-15
In place of the Psalm, an Alleluia Verse may be used.	(Psalm 118:24) On this day the Lord has acted;* we will rejoice and be glad in it.	When the chief priests had assembled with the elders and taken counsel, they gave a sum of money to the soldiers and said, Tell people, "His disciples came by night and stole him away while we were asleep."
	Alleluia

As on Monday | John 20:11-18

Mary Magdelene saw Jesus standing, but she did not know that it was Jesus. Supposing him to be the gardener, she said to him, Sir, if you have carried him away, tell me where. Jesus said to her, Mary. She turned and said to him in Hebrew, Rabboni! |
| | Alleluia

As on Monday | Luke 24:13-35

Two of the disciples were going to . . . Emmaus. When he was at table with them, he took the bread and blessed, and broke it, and gave it to them. Their eyes were opened and they recognized him. |

	FIRST LESSON	PSALM
Year ABC Thursday in Easter Week Hymn 94	**Acts 3:11–26** Peter addressed the people. You denied the Holy and Righteous One, and asked for a murderer to be granted to you, and killed the Author of life, whom God raised from the dead.	**Psalm 8** or **Psalm 114** or **Refrain:** Hallelujah! *Psalm 8* 1,2/4,5/6,7 or **Refrain:** Hallelujah! *Psalm 114* 1,2/3,4/5,6/7,8 or *Psalm 118 as on Monday*
Year ABC Friday in Easter Week Hymn 437 (tune 391)	**Acts 4:1–12** The priests and the captain of the temple and the Sadducees arrested them. Peter, filled with the Holy Spirit, said, Rulers . . . be it known to you all . . . that by the name of Jesus Christ . . . this man is standing before you well.	**Psalm 116:1–8** or **Refrain:** Hallelujah! *Psalm 116* 1/2,3/5,6/7,8 or *Psalm 118 as on Monday*
Year ABC Saturday in Easter Week Hymn 99	**Acts 4:13–21** They saw the boldness of Peter and John . . . and charged them not to speak. Peter and John answered them . . . We cannot but speak of what we have seen and heard.	**Psalm 118:14–18** or **Refrain:** Hallelujah! *Psalm 118* 1,14/15,16/17,18 or *Psalm 118 as on Monday*

In place of the Psalm, an Alleluia Verse may be used.	**Alleluia**	**Luke 24:36b–48**

As on Monday

Jesus himself stood among them. But they were startled and frightened, and supposed that they saw a spirit. See my hands and my feet, that it is I myself; handle me and see. Then he opened their minds to understand the scriptures.

Alleluia

As on Monday

John 21:1–14

Jesus revealed himself again to the disciples by the Sea of Tiberias. He said, Cast the net on the right side of the boat. Peter . . . hauled the net ashore, full of large fish, a hundred and fifty-three of them.

Alleluia

As on Monday

Mark 16:9–15,20

When Jesus rose early on the first day of the week, he appeared to Mary Magdelene. Afterward he appeared to the eleven. He upbraided them for their unbelief and hardness of heart, because they had not believed those who saw him. Go into all the world and preach the gospel.

In Easter Season a Reading from the Acts of the Apostles normally takes the place of an Old Testament Lesson.

OTHER SUGGESTED HYMNS	FIRST LESSON	PSALM
Year B 2 of Easter (The Sunday of Thomas) Hymn 99	**Acts 3:12a,13–15,17–26** What God foretold by . . . the prophets, that his Christ should suffer, he thus fulfilled. *or* **Isaiah 26:2–9,19** The dead shall live, their bodies shall rise.	**Psalm 118:19–24** *or* **Psalm 111** *or* **Refrain:** Give thanks to the Lord, for he is good; his mercy endures for ever. *or* Hallelujah! *Psalm 118* 19,20/21,22/23,24 *or* **Refrain:** Hallelujah! *Psalm 111* 1,2/3,4/9,10
Year B 3 of Easter Hymn 207	**Acts 4:5–12** This is the stone . . . rejected by you builders, but which has become the head of the corner. *or* **Micah 4:1–5** He shall judge between many peoples . . . and they shall beat their swords into plowshares.	**Psalm 98:1–5** *or* **Refrain:** Sing to the Lord a new song. *or* Hallelujah! *Psalm 98* 1,2/3,4/5,6

The Gospels for the first three Sundays of Easter present the principal resurrection narratives. Good Shepherd Sunday is now the fourth Sunday of the season. The rest of the Sundays of Easter take their Gospels from the Johannine discourses.

SECOND LESSON	ALLELUIA	GOSPEL
1 John 5:1–6	Alleluia	John 20:19–31
Who is it that overcomes the world but he who believes that Jesus is the Son of God? or Acts 3:12a,13–15,17–26	(John 20:29) You believe in me, Thomas, because you have seen me;* blessed are those who have not seen and yet believe.	Unless I see in his hands the print of the nails . . . I will not believe. Blessed are those who have not seen and yet believe.
1 John 1:1—2:2	Alleluia	Luke 24:36b–48
We have an advocate with the Father, Jesus Christ the righteous; and he is the expiation for our sins, and . . . the sins of the whole world. or Acts 4:5–12	(Luke 24:32) Open our minds, O Lord, to understand the Scriptures;* make our hearts burn within us when you speak.	These are my words which I spoke to you . . . that everything written about me in the law of Moses and the prophets and the psalms must be fulfilled. Then he opened their minds to understand the scriptures.

Year B	**Acts 4:(23–31)32–37**	**Psalm 23**
4 of Easter	The company of those	*or* **Psalm 100**
(The Good Shepherd)	who believed were of	
	one heart and soul . . .	*or*
Hymn 345	they had everything in	**Refrain:** We are his
	common.	people and the sheep of
		his pasture.
	or **Ezek. 34:1–10**	*or* Hallelujah!
	Ho, shepherds of Israel	*Psalm 100*
	who have been feeding	1/2/3/4
	yourselves. I will rescue	
	my sheep from their	
	mouths.	

Year B	**Acts 8:26–40**	**Psalm 66:1–8**
5 of Easter	An Ethiopian was	*or*
	reading the prophet	**Refrain:** Be joyful in
Hymn 89	Isaiah. Philip . . . told	God, all you lands.
	him the good news of	*or* Hallelujah!
	Jesus. He baptized him.	*Psalm 66*
		1,2/3,4/5,6/7,8
	or **Deut. 4:32–40**	
	The Lord is God in	
	heaven above and on	
	the earth beneath; there	
	is no other.	

Year B	**Acts 11:19–30**	**Psalm 33:1–8,18–22**
6 of Easter	Those who were	*or*
	scattered because of the	**Refrain:** The
Hymn 376	persecution . . .	loving-kindness of the
Entrance Hymn 474	traveled . . . speaking	Lord fills the whole
	. . . to none except the	earth.
	Jews. Some . . . spoke	*or* Hallelujah!
	to the Greeks also. A	*Psalm 33*
	great number . . .	6,7/8,9/18,19/20,21
	turned to the Lord.	
	or **Isaiah**	
	45:11–13,18–19	
	I made the earth, and	
	created man upon it. I	
	have aroused him in	
	righteousness . . . he	
	shall build my city.	

SECOND LESSON	ALLELUIA	GOSPEL

1 John 3:1-8

See what love the Father has given us, that we should be called children of God.

or **Acts 4:(23-31)32-37**

Alleluia

(John 10:14) I am the good shepherd, says the Lord;* I know my sheep, and my sheep know me.

John 10:11-16

The good shepherd lays down his life for the sheep. I am the good shepherd.

---

1 John 3:(14-17)18-24

This is his commandment, that we should believe in the name of his Son Jesus Christ and love one another.

or **Acts 8:26-40**

Alleluia

(John 14:23) If anyone loves me, he will keep my word;* and my Father will love him, and we will come to him.

John 14:15-21

If you love me, you will keep my commandments. And I will pray the Father, and he will give you another Counselor, to be with you for ever.

---

1 John 4:7-21

We love, because he first loved us. If anyone says, I love God, and hates his brother, he is a liar.

or **Acts 11:19-30**

Alleluia

(John 13:34) A new commandment I give to you:* Love one another as I have loved you.

John 15:9-17

As the Father has loved me, so have I loved you. Greater love has no man than this, that a man lay down his life for his friends.

	FIRST LESSON	PSALM
Year B Ascension Day Hymn 104	**Acts 1:1–11** Men of Galilee, why do you stand looking into heaven? *or* **Ezekiel 1:3–5a,15–22,26–28** Above the firmament over their heads there was the likeness of a throne . . . seated above the likeness of a throne was a likeness as it were of a human form.	**Psalm 110:1–5** *or* **Psalm 47** *or* **Refrain** (Matt. 28:20): I am with you always, to the close of the age. *or* Hallelujah! *Psalm 110* 1/2/3/4 *or* **Refrain:** God has gone up with a shout, the Lord with the sound of the ram's-horn. *or* Hallelujah! *Psalm 47* 1,2/5,6/7,8
Year B 7 of Easter Hymn 106	**Acts 1:15–26** One of the men who has accompanied us must become with us a witness to his resurrection. The lot fell on Matthias. *or* **Exodus 28:1–4,9–10,29–30** Aaron shall bear the judgment of the people of Israel upon his heart before the Lord continually.	**Psalm 47** *or* **Psalm 68:1–20** *or* **Refrain:** God has gone up with a shout, the Lord with the sound of the ram's-horn. *or* Hallelujah! *Psalm 47* 1,2/5,6/7,8 *or* **Refrain:** Sing to God, O kingdoms of the earth; sing praises to the Lord. *or* Hallelujah! *Psalm 68* 4,5/7,8/17,18

Ephesians 1:15–23

The riches of his glorious inheritance in the saints . . . which he accomplished in Christ when he raised him from the dead.

or **Acts 1:1–11**

Alleluia

(Matt. 28:19,20) Go and make disciples of all nations;* I am with you always, to the close of the age.

Luke 24:49–53

While he blessed them, he parted from them, and was carried up into heaven.

or **Mark 16:9–15,19–20** The Lord Jesus . . . was taken up into heaven, and sat down at the right hand of God.

---

1 John 5:9–15

This is the testimony, that God gave us eternal life, and this life is in his Son. He who has the Son has life; he who has not the Son of God has not life.

or **Acts 1:15–26**

Alleluia

(John 14:18) The Lord said, I will not leave you desolate;* I will come back to you, and your hearts will rejoice.

John 17:11b–19

That they may be one, even as we are one. Sanctify them in the truth; thy word is truth. As thou didst send me into the world, so I have sent them into the world.

	FIRST LESSON	PSALM
Year ABC	**Genesis 11:1–9**	**Psalm 33:12–22**
Vigil of Pentecost	*The Tower of Babel*	*or*
or		**Refrain:** Happy is the nation whose God is the Lord.
Early Service		*Psalm 33* 13,14,15/16,18,19/20,21,22
	Exodus 19:1–9,16–20a, 20:18–20	**Canticle 2 or 13**
		or
	The Covenant	**Refrain** (Exod. 19:6): He has made us a kingdom of priests and a holy nation.
		Canticle 13 1,2/3,4/5,6
	Ezekiel 37:1–14	**Psalm 130**
	The valley of dry bones	*or*
		Refrain: With the Lord there is mercy; with him there is plenteous redemption.
		Psalm 130 1/2,3/4,5/6,7
	Joel 2:28–32	**Canticle 9**
	God will pour out his Spirit	*or*
		Refrain: You shall draw water with rejoicing from the springs of salvation.
		Canticle 9 1,2/4,5/6,7
	Acts 2:1–11	**Psalm 104:25–32**
	The story of Pentecost	*or*
		Refrain: Send forth your Spirit, O Lord, and renew the face of the earth.
		or Hallelujah!
		Psalm 104 25,26/28,29/30,31/32,35

SECOND LESSON	ALLELUIA	GOSPEL
Romans 8:14–17,22–27	**Alleluia**	**John 7:37–39a**
All who are led by the Spirit of God are sons of God. *or* **Acts 2:1–11**	Come, Holy Spirit, and fill the hearts of your faithful people,* and kindle in them the fire of your love.	If any one thirst, let him come to me and drink. This he said about the Spirit.

It is appropriate that the Gospel be read several times, each time in a different language.

	FIRST LESSON	PSALM
Year B	**Acts 2:1–11**	**Psalm 104:25–32**
The Day of Pentecost		*or* **Psalm**
Principal Service	When the day of	**33:12–15,18–22**
	Pentecost had come,	
Hymn 109	they were all together in	*or*
	one place.	**Refrain:** Send forth
		your Spirit, O Lord,
	or **Isaiah 44:1–8**	and renew the face or
	I will pour my Spirit	the earth.
	upon your descendants,	*or* Hallelujah!
	and my blessing on	*Psalm 104*
	your offspring.	25,26/28,29/30,31/32,35
Year B	**Exodus 3:1–6**	**Canticle 2 or 13**
Trinity Sunday		*or* **Psalm 93**
Hymn 285	I am the God of your	
	father, the God of	*or*
	Abraham, the God of	**Refrain:** Glory to you,
	Isaac, and the God of	Father, Son, and Holy
	Jacob.	Spirit.
		Canticle 13
		1,2/3,4/5,6
		or
		Refrain (Exod. 15:18):
		The Lord shall reign for
		ever and for ever.
		Psalm 93
		1,2/3,4/5,6

SECOND LESSON	ALLELUIA	GOSPEL
1 Cor. 12:4–13	**Alleluia**	**John 20:19–23**
To each is given the manifestation of the Spirit for the common good.	Come, Holy Spirit, and fill the hearts of your faithful people,* and kindle in them the fire of your love.	Receive the Holy Spirit. If you forgive the sins of any, they are forgiven.
or **Acts 2:1–11**		*or* **John 14:8–17** If you love me, you will keep my commandments. And I will pray the Father, and he will give you another Counselor, to be with you for ever.
Romans 8:12–17	**Alleluia**	**John 3:1–16**
When we cry, Abba! Father! it is the Spirit himself bearing witness with our spirit that we are children of God . . . then heirs, heirs of God and fellow heirs with Christ.	(Rev. 1:4) Glory to the Father and to the Son and to the Holy Spirit:* to God who is, and who was, and who is to come.	Unless one is born of water and the Spirit, he cannot enter the kingdom of God.

The Gospels for the Sundays after Pentecost in Year B continue the reading of the Gospel according to Mark begun on the Sundays after Epiphany. The Second Lessons consist of semi-continuous readings from 2 Corinthians, Ephesians, James, and Hebrews. The Old Testament Lessons are chosen to match the Gospel (or, occasionally the Epistle).

SEE PAGES 202–205 FOR OTHER SUGGESTED

HYMNS	FIRST LESSON	PSALM
Year B	**2 Kings 5:1–15ab**	**Psalm 42:1–7**
Proper 1	Elisha sent a messenger to Naaman the Syrian saying, Go and wash in the Jordan seven times.	or **Refrain:** As the deer longs for the water-brooks, so longs my soul for you, O God. *Psalm 42* 2,3/4,5/6,7
Closest to May 11		
Hymn 517 or 424		
Year B	**Isaiah 43:18–25**	**Psalm 32:1–8**
Proper 2	Behold, I am doing a new thing. I am He who blots out your transgressions . . . and I will not remember your sins.	or **Refrain:** Happy are they whose transgressions are forgiven, and whose sin is put away. *Psalm 32* 3,4/5,6/7,8
Closest to May 18		
Hymn 567		
Year B	**Hosea 2:14–23**	**Psalm 103:1–6**
Proper 3	In that day, says the Lord, you will call me "My husband." I will betroth you to me for ever.	or **Refrain:** The Lord is full of compassion and mercy, slow to anger and of great kindness. *Psalm 103* 1,2/3,4/5,6
Closest to May 25		
Hymn 479		

SECOND LESSON	ALLELUIA	GOSPEL
1 Cor. 9:24–27	**Alleluia**	**Mark 1:40–45**
Do you not know that in a race all the runners compete, but only one receives the prize? So run that you may obtain it.	*Ad libitum* *(See page 206)*	A leper came to Jesus. Moved with pity he stretched out his hand and touched him . . . the leprosy left him.
2 Cor. 1:18–22	**Alleluia**	**Mark 2:1–12**
All the promises of God find their Yes in him (Jesus).	*Ad libitum*	The Son of man has authority on earth to forgive sins. Rise . . . walk.
2 Cor. 3:(4–11)17—4:2	**Alleluia**	**Mark 2:18–22**
Now the Lord is the Spirit, and where the Spirit of the Lord is, there is freedom.	*Ad libitum*	Can the wedding guests fast while the bridegroom is with them? The days will come, when the bridegroom is taken away from them, and then they will fast in that day.

	FIRST LESSON	PSALM
Year B Proper 4 Closest to June 1 Hymn 195	**Deut. 5:6–21** Observe the Sabbath Day, to keep it holy.	**Psalm 81:1–10** *or* **Refrain:** Sing with joy to God our strength. *Psalm 81* *2,3/4,5/8,9/10*
Year B Proper 5 Closest to June 8 Hymn 384 or 343	**Genesis 3:(1–7)8–21** The Lord God said to the serpent . . . I will put enmity between you and the woman, and between your seed and her seed.	**Psalm 130** *or* **Refrain:** With the Lord there is mercy; with him there is plenteous redemption. *Psalm 130* *1/2,3/4,5/6,7*
Year B Proper 6 Closest to June 15 Hymn 401 or 308	**Ezek. 31:1–6,10–14** Say to Pharaoh: I will liken you to a cedar in Lebanon. The birds of the air made their nests in its boughs. Because its heart was proud of its height . . . I have cast it out.	**Psalm 92:1–4,11–14** *or* **Refrain:** The righteous shall flourish like a palm tree. *Psalm 92* *1,2/3,4/11,12/13,14*
Year B Proper 7 Closest to June 22 Hymn 298	**Job 38:1–11,16–18** The Lord answered Job out of the whirlwind. Who shut in the sea with doors, when it burst forth from the womb?	**Psalm 107:1–3,23–32** *or* **Refrain:** Give thanks to the Lord, for he is good, and his mercy endures for ever. *Psalm 107* *2,3/23,24/25,26/28,* *29/30,31*

SECOND LESSON	ALLELUIA	GOSPEL
2 Cor. 4:5–12	**Alleluia**	**Mark 2:23–28**
We are always carrying in the body the death of Jesus, so that the life of Jesus may also be manifested in our bodies.	*Ad libitum*	Jesus said, The sabbath was made for man, not man for the sabbath; so the Son of man is lord even of the sabbath.
2 Cor. 4:13–18	**Alleluia**	**Mark 3:20–35**
We do not lose heart . . . because we look not to the things that are seen but to the things that are unseen; for the things that are seen are transient, but the things that are unseen are eternal.	*Ad libitum*	How can Satan cast out Satan? If a kingdom is divided against itself, that kingdom cannot stand.
2 Cor. 5:1–10	**Alleluia**	**Mark 4:26–34**
Whether we are at home or away, we make it our aim to please him. For we must all appear before the judgment seat of Christ.	*Ad libitum*	The kingdom of God is like a grain of mustard seed . . . it grows up and becomes the greatest of all shrubs, and puts forth large branches, so that the birds of the air can make nests in its shade.
2 Cor. 5:14–21	**Alleluia**	**Mark 4:35–41; (5:1–20)**
The love of Christ controls us, because we are convinced that one has died for all. Therefore, if anyone is in Christ, he is a new creation.	*Ad libitum*	Jesus awoke and rebuked the wind, and said to the sea, Peace! Be still! And the wind ceased and there was great calm. Who then is this, that even wind and sea obey him?

	FIRST LESSON	PSALM
Year B Proper 8 Closest to June 29 Hymn 301	**Deut. 15:7–11** If there is among you a poor man . . . you shall not harden your heart . . . but you shall open your hand. You shall give it to him freely.	**Psalm 112** *of* **Refrain:** Happy are they who have given to the poor. *Psalm 112* 1,2/3,4/5,6/7,9
Year B Proper 9 Closest to July 6 Hymn 286 or 320	**Ezekiel 2:1–7** Whether they hear or refuse to hear (for they are a rebellious house) they will know that there has been a prophet among them.	**Psalm 123** *or* **Refrain:** Our eyes look to the Lord our God, pleading for his mercy. *Psalm 123* 1,2/4,5
Year B Proper 10 Closest to July 13 Hymn 131 or 380	**Amos 7:7–15** Then Amos answered, I am no prophet, nor a prophet's son. The Lord took me from following the flock, and the Lord said to me, Go, prophesy to my people Israel.	**Psalm 85:7–13** *or* **Refrain:** Show us your mercy, O Lord, and grant us your salvation. *Psalm 85* 8,9/10,11/12,13
Year B Proper 11 Closest to July 20 Hymn 345	**Isaiah 57:14b–21** I dwell in the high and holy place, and also with him who is of a contrite and humble spirit. I will not always be angry. There is no peace, says my God, for the wicked.	**Psalm 22:22–30** *or* **Refrain:** Those who seek the Lord shall praise him. *Psalm 22* 22,23/25,26/27,28/29,30

SECOND LESSON	ALLELUIA	GOSPEL
2 Cor. 8:1–9,13–15	**Alleluia**	**Mark 5:22–24,35b–43**
You know the grace of our Lord Jesus Christ . . . for your sake he became poor . . . so that you might become rich. As a matter of equality your abundance at the present time should supply their want.	*Ad libitum*	My little daughter is at the point of death. Taking her by the hand he said to her, Little girl, I say to you, arise.
2 Cor. 12:2–10	**Alleluia**	**Mark 6:1–6**
A thorn was given me in the flesh. I besought the Lord about this . . . he said to me, My grace is sufficient for you, for my power is made perfect in weakness.	*Ad libitum*	Jesus said, A prophet is not without honor, except in his own country, and among his own kin, and in his own house.
Eph. 1:1–14	**Alleluia**	**Mark 6:7–13**
He has made known to us in all wisdom and insight the mystery of his will, according to his purpose which he set forth in Christ as a plan . . . to unite all things to him.	*Ad libitum*	Jesus called to him the twelve, and began to send them out two by two. So they went out and preached that men should repent.
Eph. 2:11–22	**Alleluia**	**Mark 6:30–44**
Now in Christ Jesus you who were once far off have been brought near in the blood of Christ. For he is our peace, who has made us both one, and has broken down the dividing wall of hostility.	*Ad libitum*	As Jesus went ashore he saw a great throng, and he had compassion on them, because they were like sheep without a shepherd; and he began to teach them.

	FIRST LESSON	PSALM
Year B	**2 Kings 2:1–15**	**Psalm 114**
Proper 12	Elijah said to Elisha, Ask what I shall do for you, before I am taken from you. "I pray you, let me inherit a double share of your spirit." He took up the mantle of Elijah. The spirit of Elijah rests on Elisha.	*or* **Refrain:** Tremble, O earth, at the presence of the Lord. *Psalm 114* 1,2/3,4/5,6/7,8
Closest to July 27		
Hymn 220 or 575		
Year B	**Exodus 16:2–4,9–15**	**Psalm 78:14–20,23–25**
Proper 13	The Lord said to Moses, Behold, I will rain bread from heaven for you.	*or* **Refrain:** The Lord rained down manna from heaven. *Psalm 78* 14,15/17,18/19,23/24,25
Closest to August 3		
Hymn 213 or 385		
Year B	**Deut. 8:1–10**	**Psalm 34:1–8**
Proper 14	The Lord your God has led you these forty years in the wilderness . . . fed you with manna . . . that he might make you know that man does not live by bread alone.	*or* **Refrain:** Taste and see that the Lord is good. *Psalm 34* 1,2/3,4/5,6/7,8
Closest to August 10		
Hymn 192		
Year B	**Proverbs 9:1–6**	**Psalm 34:9–14** *or* **Psalm 147**
Proper 15	Wisdom says, Come eat of my bread and drink of the wine I have mixed. Leave simpleness, and live and walk in the way of insight.	*or* **Refrain:** Taste and see that the Lord is good. *Psalm 34* 9,10/11,12/13,14
Closest to August 17		
Hymn 197		

SECOND LESSON	ALLELUIA	GOSPEL
Eph. 4:1–7,11–16	**Alleluia**	**Mark 6:45–52**
Lead a life worthy of the calling to which you have been called . . . And his gifts were that some should be apostles, some prophets, some evangelists, some pastors and teachers, to equip the saints for the work of ministry.	*Ad libitum*	Jesus came to them, walking on the sea. He said, Take heart, it is I; have no fear. The wind ceased. And they were utterly astounded, for they did not understand about the loaves.
Eph. 4:17–25	**Alleluia**	**John 6:24–35**
You must no longer live as the Gentiles do . . . they are darkened in their understanding, alienated from the life of God. Put on the new nature, created after the likeness of God.	*Ad libitum*	I am the bread of life; he who comes to me shall not hunger, and he who believes in me shall never thirst.
Eph. 4:(25–29)30—5:2	**Alleluia**	**John 6:37–51**
Walk in love, as Christ loved us and gave himself up for us, a fragrant offering and sacrifice to God.	*Ad libitum*	I am the living bread which came down from heaven; if any one eats of this bread, he will live for ever; and the bread which I shall give for the life of the world is my flesh.
Eph. 5:15–20	**Alleluia**	**John 6:53–59**
Look carefully then how you walk, not as unwise men but as wise. Understand what the will of the Lord is.	*Ad libitum*	My flesh is food indeed, and my blood is drink indeed. As the living Father sent me, and I live because of the Father, so he who eats me will live because of me.

	FIRST LESSON	PSALM
Year B Proper 16 Closest to August 24 Hymn 210 or 551	Joshua 24:1–2a,14–25 The people answered, Far be it from us that we should forsake the Lord, to serve other gods; for it is the Lord our God who brought us and our fathers up from the land of Egypt . . . we also will serve the Lord, for he is our God.	Psalm 34:15–22 or Psalm 16 or Refrain: Taste and see that the Lord is good. *Psalm 34* 15,16/17,18/19,20/21,22
Year B Proper 17 Closest to August 31 Hymn 500	Deut. 4:1–9 You shall not add to the word which I command you. Keep them and do them, for that will be your wisdom and your understanding.	Psalm 15 or Refrain: The righteous shall abide upon God's holy hill *Psalm 15* 1,2/3,4/5,6/7
Year B Proper 18 Closest to Sept. 7 Hymn 325	Isaiah 35:4–7a The eyes of the blind shall be opened, and the ears of the deaf unstopped.	Psalm 146:4–9 or Refrain: Praise the Lord, O my soul. *Psalm 146* 4,5/6,7/8,9

SECOND LESSON	ALLELUIA	GOSPEL
Eph. 5:21–33	**Alleluia**	**John 6:60–69**
Christ loved the church and gave himself up for her, that he might sanctify her. This mystery is a profound one.	*Ad libitum*	Jesus said to the twelve, Do you also wish to go away? Simon Peter answered him, Lord, to whom shall we go? You have the words of eternal life.
Eph. 6:10–20	**Alleluia**	**Mark 7:1–8,14–15,21–23**
Put on the whole armor of God, that you may be able to stand against the wiles of the devil.	*Ad libitum*	This people honors me with their lips, but their heart is far from me; in vain do they worship me; teaching as doctrines the precepts of men.
James 1:17–27	**Alleluia**	**Mark 7:31–37**
Be doers of the word, and not hearers only, deceiving yourselves.	*Ad libitum*	Jesus said, Ephphatha. The deaf man's ears were opened, his tongue was released, and he spoke plainly. He even makes the deaf hear and the dumb (mute) speak.

	FIRST LESSON	PSALM
Year B	**Isaiah 50:4–9**	**Psalm 116:1–8**
Proper 19	I gave my back to the smiters, and my cheeks to those who pulled out the beard; I hid not my face from shame and spitting.	*or* **Refrain:** I will walk in the presence of the Lord in the land of the living. *Psalm 116* 1/2,3/4,5/6,7
Closest to Sept. 14		
Hymn 337		
Year B	**Wisdom 1:16—2:1(6–11)12–22**	**Psalm 54**
Proper 20	Let us test him with insult and torture. Let us condemn him to a shameful death, for, according to what he says, he will be protected.	*or* **Refrain:** God is my helper; the Lord sustains my life. *Psalm 54* 1,2/3,5/6,7
Closest to Sept. 21		
Hymn 75 or 335		
Year B	**Numbers 11:4–6,10–16,24–29**	**Psalm 19:7–14**
Proper 21	A young man ran and told Moses, Eldad and Medad are prophesying. Joshua said . . . Forbid them. Moses said . . . Are you jealous for my sake? Would that all the Lord's people were prophets.	*or* **Refrain:** The statutes of the Lord rejoice the heart. *Psalm 19* 7,8/9,10/11,12/13,14
Closest to Sept. 28		
Hymn 536		

SECOND LESSON	ALLELUIA	GOSPEL
James 2:1–5,8–10,14–18 Has not God chosen those who are poor in the world to be rich in faith . . . What does it profit, my brethren, if a man says he has faith but has not works? Faith by itself, if it has no works, is dead.	**Alleluia** *Ad libitum*	**Mark 8:27–38** Jesus began to teach the disciples that the Son of man must suffer many things, and be rejected by the elders and the chief priests and the scribes, and be killed, and after three days rise again. *or* **Mark 9:14–29** Lord I believe, help thou my unbelief.
James 3:16—4:6 Where jealousy and selfish ambition exist, there will be disorder and every vile practice.	**Alleluia** *Ad libitum*	**Mark 9:30–37** The Son of man will be delivered into the hands of men, and they will kill him; and when he is killed, after three days he will rise.
James 4:7–12(13—5:6) Humble yourselves before the Lord and he will exalt you. There is one law-giver and judge, he who is able to save and to destroy. But who are you that you judge your neighbor?	**Alleluia** *Ad libitum*	**Mark** 9:38–43,45,47–48 John said to Jesus, Teacher, we saw a man casting out demons in your name and we forbade him. Jesus said, Do not forbid him. He that is not against us is for us.

	FIRST LESSON	PSALM
Year B	**Genesis 2:18–24**	**Psalm 128**
Proper 22	A man leaves his father	*or* **Psalm 8**
Closest to Oct. 5	and mother and cleaves	*or*
Hymn 277	to his wife, and they become one flesh.	**Refrain:** May the Lord bless you from Zion all the days of your life. *Psalm 128* 1,2/3,4/5,6
		or **Refrain:** O Lord our Governor, how exalted is your Name in all the world. *Psalm 8* 4,5/6,7/8,9
Year B	**Amos 5:6–7,10–15**	**Psalm 90:1–8,12**
Proper 23	Seek good, and not	*or*
Closest to Oct. 12	evil, that you may live; and so the Lord, the	**Refrain:** Teach us to number our days that
Hymn 532 or 258	God of hosts, will be with you.	we may apply our hearts to wisdom. *Psalm 90* 1,2/3,4/5,6/7,8
Year B	**Isaiah 53:4–12**	**Psalm 91:9–16**
Proper 24	It was the will of the	*or*
Closest to Oct. 19	Lord to bruise him; he has put him to grief;	**Refrain:** Because he is bound to me in love,
Hymn 344	when he makes himself an offering for sin, he shall see his offspring, he shall prolong his days.	therefore will I deliver him. *Psalm 91* 9,10/11,12/13,14/15,16

SECOND LESSON	ALLELUIA	GOSPEL
Hebrews 2:(1–8)9–18	**Alleluia**	**Mark 10:2–9**
He had to be made like his brethren in every respect, so that he might become a merciful and faithful high priest in the service of God, to make expiation for the sins of the people.	*Ad libitum*	Is it lawful for a man to divorce his wife? Jesus said . . . From the beginning of creation, God made them male and female. What therefore God has joined together, let not man put asunder.
Hebrews 3:1–6	**Alleluia**	**Mark 10:17–27(28–31)**
Christ was faithful over God's house as a son. We are his house if we hold fast our confidence and pride in our hope.	*Ad libitum*	Go, sell what you have, give to the poor . . . and come, follow me. The young man went away sorrowful; for he had great possessions.
Hebrews 4:12–16	**Alleluia**	**Mark 10:35–45**
The word of God is living and active . . . discerning the thoughts and intentions of the heart. We have a great high priest who has passed through the heavens.	*Ad libitum*	Jesus said to James and John, You do not know what you are asking. Are you able to drink the cup that I drink or to be baptized with the baptism with which I am baptized?

	FIRST LESSON	PSALM
Year B	**Isaiah 59:(1–4)9–19**	**Psalm 13**
Proper 25	Justice is far from us.	*or*
Closest to Oct. 26	We look for light, and behold, darkness. The	**Refrain:** Give light to my eyes, O Lord.
Hymn 293 or 347	Lord saw it, and it displeased him. His own right arm brought him victory.	*Psalm 13* 1,2/3,4/5,6/7,8
Year B	**Deut. 6:1–9**	**Psalm 119:1–8**
Proper 26	Hear, O Israel: The	*or*
Closest to Nov. 2	Lord our God is one Lord; and you shall love	**Refrain** (Ps. 18:1): I love you, O Lord my
Hymn 456 or 479	the Lord your God with all your heart, and with all your soul, and with all your might.	strength. *Psalm 119* 1,2/3,4/5,6/7,8
Year B	**1 Kings 17:8–16**	**Psalm 146:4–9**
Proper 27	The widow said, I have	*or*
Closest to Nov. 9	nothing baked, only a handful of meal . . .	**Refrain:** Praise the Lord, O my soul.
Hymn 156 or 494	and a little oil . . . for myself and my son, that we may eat it, and die. Elijah said, The jar of meal shall not be spent.	*Psalm 146* 4,5/6,7/8,9
Year B	**Daniel 12:1–4a(5–13)**	**Psalm 16:5–11**
Proper 28	At that time shall arise	*or*
Closest to Nov. 16	Michael. There shall be a time of trouble . . .	**Refrain:** The Lord will show me the path of
Hymn 396 or 468	but at that time your people shall be delivered, every one whose name shall be found written in the book.	life. *Psalm 16* 5,6/7,8/9,10/11

SECOND LESSON	ALLELUIA	GOSPEL
Hebrews 5:12—6:1,9–12 God is not so unjust as to overlook your work and the love which you showed for his sake in serving the saints.	**Alleluia** *Ad libitum*	**Mark 10:46–52** Bartimaeus cried out, Son of David, have mercy on me. Jesus said . . . Go your way; your faith has made you well.
Hebrews 7:23–28 The former priests were many in number, because they were prevented by death from continuing in office; but Christ holds his priesthood permanently.	**Alleluia** *Ad libitum*	**Mark 12:28–34** The scribe said to Jesus, You are right, Teacher; you have truly said that . . . to love him . . . and to love one's neighbor . . . is much more than all . . . sacrifices. Jesus said, You are not far from the kingdom of God.
Hebrews 9:24–28 Christ, having been offered once to bear the sins of many, will appear a second time, not to deal with sin but to save those who are eagerly waiting for him.	**Alleluia** (Matt. 24:42,44) Be watchful and ready,* for you know not when the Son of Man is coming.	**Mark 12:38–44** Truly, I say to you, this poor widow has put in more than all those who are contributing to the treasury. She out of her poverty has put in everything she had.
Hebrews 10:31–39 The coming one shall come and shall not tarry; but my righteous one shall live by faith.	**Alleluia** (Rev. 2:10) Be faithful until death, says the Lord,* and I will give you the crown of life.	**Mark 13:14–23** False Christs and false prophets will arise and show signs and wonders, to lead astray, if possible, the elect.

	FIRST LESSON	PSALM
Year B	**Daniel 7:9–14**	**Psalm 93**
Proper 29	There came one like a	*or*
Closest to Nov. 23	son of man. His	**Refrain** (Exod. 15:18):
(Christ the King)	dominion is an	The Lord shall reign for
	everlasting dominion	ever and for ever.
Hymn 522 or 106	. . . and his kingdom	*Psalm 93*
	one that shall not be	1,2/3,4/5,6
	destroyed.	

SECOND LESSON	ALLELUIA	GOSPEL
Revelation 1:1–8	**Alleluia**	**John 18:33–37**
The ruler of kings on earth . . . made us a kingdom, priests to his God and Father.	(Mark 11:10) Blessed is the kingdom of our father David that is coming;* blessed is he who comes in the name of the Lord.	My kingship is not of this world; if my kingship were of this world, my servants would fight.
		or **Mark 11:1–11** Blessed be he who comes in the name of the Lord.

Year C

The themes of the Advent Sundays are the same in all three years.

SEE PAGES 202–205 FOR
OTHER SUGGESTED
HYMNS

	FIRST LESSON	PSALM
Year C 1 Advent (The final Advent) Hymn 5	**Zech. 14:4–9** The Lord will become king over all the earth; on that day the Lord will be one and his name one.	**Psalm 50:1–6** *or* **Refrain:** Out of Zion, perfect in its beauty, God reveals himself in glory. *Psalm 50* 1,2/3,4/5,6
Year C 2 Advent (The Ministry of John the Baptist) Hymn 10	**Baruch 5:1–9** God will lead Israel with joy, in the light of his glory, with the mercy and righteousness that come from him.	**Psalm 126** *or* **Refrain:** The Lord has done great things for us, and we are glad indeed. *Psalm 126* 1,2/3,4/5,6/7
Year C 3 Advent (The Ministry of John the Baptist) Hymn 4	**Zeph. 3:14–20** Sing aloud, O daughter of Zion. Rejoice and exult with all your heart. The Lord, your God, is in your midst . . . he will renew you in his love.	**Canticle 9** *or* **Psalm 85:7–13** *or* **Refrain:** Ring out your joy, inhabitants of Zion; the Holy One of Israel is in the midst of you. *Canticle 9* 1,2/3,4/5,6 *or* **Refrain:** Show us your mercy, O Lord, and grant us your salvation. *Psalm 85* 8,9/10,11/12,13

SECOND LESSON	ALLELUIA	GOSPEL
1 Thess. 3:9–13	**Alleluia**	**Luke 21:25–31**
May our God and Father . . . establish your hearts . . . in holiness before . . . the coming of our Lord Jesus with all his saints.	(Psalm 85:7) Show us your mercy, O Lord,* and grant us your salvation.	There will be signs in the sun and moon and stars. The Son of man coming in a cloud with power and great glory.
Phil. 1:1–11	**Alleluia**	**Luke 3:1–6**
He who began a good work in you will bring it to completion at the day of Jesus Christ.	(Luke 3:4,6) Prepare the way of the Lord, make his paths straight;* and all flesh shall see the salvation of our God.	The voice of one crying in the wilderness: Prepare the way of the Lord.
Phil. 4:4–7(8–9)	**Alleluia**	**Luke 3:7–18**
Rejoice in the Lord always. The Lord is at hand. Have no anxiety.	(Luke 4:18) The Spirit of the Lord is upon me;* he has anointed me to preach good tidings to the poor.	I baptize you with water; but he who is mightier . . . is coming . . . he will baptize you with the Holy Spirit and with fire.

	FIRST LESSON	PSALM
Year C 4 Advent (The Annunciation) Hymn 2	**Micah 5:2–4** But you, O Bethlehem . . . from you shall come forth for me one who is to be ruler in Israel.	**Psalm 80:1–7** *or* **Refrain:** Restore us, O God of hosts; show the light of your countenance and we shall be saved. *Psalm 80* 1,2/4,14/16,17
Year ABC Christmas Day I (At Midnight) Hymn 20 or 42	**Isaiah 9:2–4,6–7** The people who walked in darkness have seen a great light. For to us a child is born . . . and the government will be upon his shoulder.	**Psalm 96:1–4,11–12** *or* **Refrain** (Luke 2:11): Today is born our Savior, Christ the Lord. *Psalm 96* 1,2/3,4/11,12
Year ABC Christmas Day II (At Dawn) Hymn 13	**Isaiah 62:6–7,10–12** Say to the daughter of Zion, Behold, your salvation comes. They shall be called The holy people, The redeemed of the Lord.	**Psalm 97:1–4,11–12** *or* **Refrain** (Isa. 9:6): To us a child is born; to us a Son is given. *Psalm 97* 1,2/3,4/11,12
Year ABC Christmas Day III (During the Day) Hymn 18	**Isaiah 52:7–10** How beautiful upon the mountains are the feet of him who brings good tidings. All the ends of the earth shall see the salvation of our God.	**Psalm 98:1–6** *or* **Refrain:** All the ends of the earth have seen the salvation of our God. *Psalm 98* 1,2/3,4/5,6

SECOND LESSON	ALLELUIA	GOSPEL
Hebrews 10:5–10	**Alleluia**	**Luke 1:39–49(50–56)**
Sacrifices and offerings thou hast not desired, but a body hast thou prepared for me.	(Luke 1:38) Behold, I am the handmaid of the Lord;* let it be to me according to your word.	Blessed are you among women, and blessed is the fruit of your womb! My soul magnifies the Lord.
Titus 2:11–14	**Alleluia**	**Luke 2:1–14(15–20)**
The grace of God has appeared for the salvation of all . . . the appearing of the glory of our great God and Savior Jesus Christ.	(Luke 2:10,11) Behold, I bring you good tidings of great joy;* to you is born a Savior, Christ the Lord.	To you is born this day in the city of David a Savior, who is Christ the Lord.
Titus 3:4–7	**Alleluia**	**Luke 2:(1–14)15–20**
He saved us . . . by the washing of regeneration and renewal in the Holy Spirit.	(Luke 2:14) Glory to God in the highest,* and peace to his people on earth.	Let us go over to Bethlehem and see this thing that has happened, which the Lord has made known to us.
Hebrews 1:1–12	**Alleluia**	**John 1:1–14**
God spoke of old . . . by the prophets; but in these last days he has spoken to us by a Son . . . through whom also he created the world. Thou art my Son, today I have begotten thee.	(John 1:14) The Word was made flesh and dwelt among us,* full of grace and truth.	The Word became flesh and dwelt among us, full of grace and truth.

	FIRST LESSON	PSALM
Year ABC First Sunday after Christmas (The Incarnation) Hymn 17	**Isaiah 61:10—62:3** The Lord God will cause righteousness and praise to spring forth before all the nations.	**Psalm 147:13–21** *or* **Refrain** (John 1:14): The Word was made flesh and dwelt among us. *Psalm 147* 13,14/15,16/20,21
Year ABC The Holy Name of our Lord Jesus Christ January 1 Hymn 326	**Exodus 34:1–8** Moses cut two tables of stone . . . and went up on Mount Sinai. The Lord descended in the cloud and stood with him there and proclaimed the name of the Lord.	**Psalm 8** *or* **Refrain:** O Lord our Governor, how exalted is your Name in all the world. *Psalm 8* 4,5/6,7/8,9
Year ABC Second Sunday after Christmas (The Holy Family) Hymn 504 or 35	**Jeremiah 31:7–14** Behold, I will bring them from the north country . . . the woman with child and her who is in travail together; a great company, they shall return here. I am a father to Israel, and Ephraim is my first-born.	**Psalm 84:1–8** *or* **Refrain:** How dear to me is your dwelling, O Lord of hosts. *Psalm 84* 1bc,2/3,4/5,6/7,8

Gal. 3:23–25; 4:4–7	**Alleluia**	**John 1:1–18**
God sent forth his Son, born of a woman, born under the law, to redeem those who were under the law, so that we might receive adoption as sons.	(John 1:14) We have seen his glory;* glory that is his as the Father's only Son.	To all who received him he gave power to become the children of God. The law was given through Moses; grace and truth came through Jesus Christ.
Romans 1:1–7	**Alleluia**	**Luke 2:15–21**
The Gospel of God which he promised beforehand through his prophets in the holy scriptures, the gospel concerning his Son, who was descended from David according to the flesh.	(Heb. 1:1,2) In the past God spoke to our fathers through the prophets,* but now he has spoken to us through his Son.	At the end of eight days, when he was circumcised, he was called Jesus, the name given by the angel before he was conceived in the womb.
Eph. 1:3–6,15–19a	**Alleluia**	**Matt. 2:13–15,19–23**
Blessed be the God and Father of our Lord Jesus Christ. He destined us in love to be his sons through Jesus Christ.	(John 1:14) The Word was made flesh and dwelt among us,* full of grace and truth.	Take the child and his mother. "Out of Egypt have I called my son."
		or **Luke 2:41–52** After three days they found him in the temple.
		or **Matt. 2:1–12** Wise men from the east came to Jerusalem, saying, Where is he who has been born king of the Jews?

	FIRST LESSON	PSALM
Year ABC The Epiphany January 6 Hymn 47	**Isaiah 60:1–6,9** Nations shall come to your light, and kings to the brightness of your rising. They shall bring gold and frankincense.	**Psalm 72:1–2,10–17** *or* **Refrain:** All kings shall bow down before him; all the nations shall do him service. *Psalm 72* 1,2/8,10/12,13/17
Year C 1 Epiphany (The Baptism of Our Lord) Hymn 545 Entrance Hymn 53	**Isaiah 42:1–9** Behold my servant, whom I uphold, my chosen, in whom my soul delights; I have put my Spirit upon him.	**Psalm 89:20–29** *or* **Refrain:** I have found David my servant; with my holy oil have I anointed him. *Psalm 89* 21,22/24,25/26,27/28,29
Year C 2 Epiphany Hymn 53	**Isaiah 62:1–5** As the bridegroom rejoices over the bride, so shall your God rejoice over you.	**Psalm 96:1–10** *or* **Refrain:** Proclaim the glory of the Lord among the nations. *Psalm 96* 1,2/3,4/7,8/9,10

SECOND LESSON	ALLELUIA	GOSPEL
Eph. 3:1–12 Grace was given to preach to the Gentiles the unsearchable riches of Christ.	**Alleluia** (Matt. 2:2) We have seen his star in the east,* and have come to worship the Lord.	**Matthew 2:1–12** Wise men from the east came to Jerusalem, saying, Where is he who has been born king of the Jews? They offered him gifts, gold and frankincense and myrrh.
Acts 10:34–38 Good news of peace by Jesus Christ . . . beginning from Galilee after the baptism which John preached: How God anointed Jesus of Nazareth with the Holy Spirit.	**Alleluia** (Gal. 3:27) All of you who were baptized into Christ* have clothed yourselves with Christ.	**Luke 3:15–16,21–22** When Jesus had been baptized and was praying, the heaven was opened, and the Holy Spirit descended upon him in bodily form, as a dove. Thou art my beloved Son; with thee I am well pleased.
1 Cor. 12:4–11 Now there are varieties of gifts, but the same Spirit.	**Alleluia** (John 2:11) Jesus manifested his glory,* and his disciples believed in him.	**John 2:1–11** There was a marriage at Cana in Galilee. The water now became wine. This, the first of his signs, Jesus did at Cana.

The Gospel Lessons for the remaining Sundays after Epiphany present the beginnings of our Lord's ministry. During Year C they are chosen from the Gospel according to Luke. The Old Testament Lessons are selected to match the Gospels. The Epistles consist of semi-continuous readings from First Corinthians which was introduced last Sunday.

SEE PAGES 202–205 FOR
OTHER SUGGESTED

HYMNS	FIRST LESSON	PSALM
Year C	**Nehemiah 8:2–10**	**Psalm 113**
3 Epiphany	Ezra the priest brought	*or*
Hymn 256 or 376	the law before the assembly. They (the Levites) read from the book, from the law of God, clearly, and they gave the sense, so that the people understood the reading.	**Refrain:** From the rising of the sun to its going down let the Name of the Lord be praised. *Psalm 113* 1,2/3,4/5,6/7,8
Year C	**Jeremiah 1:4–10**	**Psalm 71:1–6,15–17**
4 Epiphany	I appointed you a	*or*
Hymn 253	prophet to the nations. Be not afraid of them. I have put my words in your mouth.	**Refrain:** My tongue will proclaim your righteousness, O God. *Psalm 71* 1,2/3,4/5,6/15,17
Year C	**Judges 6:11–24a**	**Psalm 85:7–13**
5 Epiphany	Gideon said, Alas, O	*or*
Hymn 566 or 437 (tune 391)	Lord God. For now I have seen the angel of the Lord face to face. The Lord said to him, Peace be to you; do not fear, you shall not die.	**Refrain:** I will listen to what the Lord God is saying. *Psalm 85* 7,8/9,10/11,13

SECOND LESSON	ALLELUIA	GOSPEL
1 Cor. 12:12–27	**Alleluia**	**Luke 4:14–21**
The body is one and has many members. If one member suffers, all suffer together; if one member is honored, all rejoice together.	(Luke 4:18,19) The Lord has anointed me to preach good news to the poor,* and to set at liberty those who are oppressed.	There was given to Jesus the book of the prophet Isaiah. The Spirit of the Lord is upon me. Today this Scripture has been fulfilled in your hearing.
1 Cor. 14:12b–20	**Alleluia**	**Luke 4:21–32**
He who speaks in a tongue should pray for the power to interpret. In church I would rather speak five words with my mind, in order to instruct others, than ten thousand words in a tongue.	*Ad libitum* *(see page 206)*	No prophet is acceptable in his own country.
1 Cor. 15:1–11	**Alleluia**	**Luke 5:1–11**
I am the least of the apostles, unfit to be called an apostle. But by the grace of God I am what I am.	*Ad libitum*	They enclosed a great shoal of fish. When Simon Peter saw it, he fell down at Jesus' knees, saying, Depart from me, for I am a sinful man, O Lord. Jesus said, Do not be afraid; henceforth you will be catching men.

	FIRST LESSON	PSALM
Year C 6 Epiphany Hymn 418	**Jeremiah 17:5–10** Cursed is the man who trusts in man. Blessed is the man who trusts in the Lord.	**Psalm 1** *or* **Refrain:** Happy are they whose delight is in the law of the Lord. *Psalm 1* 1,2/3,4/5,6
Year C 7 Epiphany Hymn 298	**Gen. 45:3–11,21–28** Joseph said to his brothers, Come near to me, I pray you. Do not be distressed, or angry with yourselves. God sent me before you to preserve a remnant on earth. It was not you who sent me here, but God.	**Psalm 37:3–10** *or* **Refrain:** Put your trust in the Lord and do good. *Psalm 37* 1,3/4,5/6,7/8,10
Year C 8 Epiphany Hymn 564	**Jeremiah 7:1–7(8–15)** Do not trust in these deceptive words: This is the temple of the Lord. For if you truly amend your ways and . . . execute justice . . . then I will let you dwell in this place.	**Psalm 92:1–5,11–14** *or* **Refrain:** It is a good thing to give thanks to the Lord. *Psalm 92* 2,3/11,12/13,14

SECOND LESSON	ALLELUIA	GOSPEL
1 Cor. 15:12–20	**Alleluia**	**Luke 6:17–26**
How can some of you say that there is no resurrection of the dead? Christ has been raised from the dead.	*Ad libitum*	Blessed are you poor, for yours is the kingdom of God. Woe to you that are rich.
1 Cor. 15:35–38,42–50	**Alleluia**	**Luke 6:27–38**
Just as we have borne the image of the man of dust, we shall also bear the image of the man of heaven.	*Ad libitum*	Love your enemies . . . Do not withhold your coat. Judge not, and you will not be judged . . . forgive, and you will be forgiven.
1 Cor. 15:50–58	**Alleluia**	**Luke 6:39–49**
The sting of death is sin, and the power of sin is the law. But thanks be to God who gives us the victory through our Lord Jesus Christ.	*Ad libitum*	Why do you call me "Lord, Lord," and not do what I tell you?

Year C	**Exodus 34:29–35**	**Psalm 99**
Last Sunday After Epiphany	When Moses came down from Mount Sinai . . . Moses did not know that the skin of his face shone because he had been talking with God.	*or* **Refrain:** Proclaim the greatness of the Lord our God; he is the Holy one. *Psalm 99* 1,2/6,7/8,9
(The Transfiguration)		
Hymn 119 Dismissal Hymn 54		

Year ABC	**Joel 2:1–2,12–17**	**Psalm 103:8–14**
Ash Wednesday	Return to me with all your heart, with fasting, with weeping. Return to the Lord, your God, for he is gracious and merciful.	*or* **Refrain:** The Lord remembers that we are but dust. *Psalm 103* 8,9/10,11/12,13
Hymn 56 Dismissal Hymn 61		
	or **Isaiah 58:1–12** Cry aloud . . . declare to my people their transgression. Is not this the fast I choose: to loose the bonds of wickedness . . . to let the oppressed go free?	
Proper Liturgy, page 264		

SECOND LESSON	CHANT BEFORE GOSPEL	GOSPEL
1 Cor. 12:27—13:13 Faith, hope, love abide, these three; but the greatest of these is love.	**Alleluia** (Matt. 17:5) This is my Son, my Beloved,* with whom I am well pleased.	**Luke 9:28–36** Two men talked with Jesus, Moses and Elijah, who appeared in glory and spoke of his departure (exodus) which he was to accomplish at Jerusalem. A voice came out of a cloud, saying, This is my Son, my Chosen.
2 Cor. 5:20b—6:10 Behold, now is the acceptable time; behold, now is the day of salvation.	**Verse*** (2 Cor. 6:2) Behold, now is the acceptable time;* behold, now is the day of salvation. *or* **Tract** Psalm 130:1–4(5–7) * *See the Introduction*	**Matt. 6:1–6,16–21** Beware of practicing your piety before men in order to be seen by them; for then you will have no reward from your Father who is in heaven.

The Lessons appointed for the Season of Lent are intended as background and preparation for Easter. The Old Testament Lessons (beginning with the Second Sunday) present a synopsis of the history of salvation from the Covenant with Abraham to the promise of deliverance from the exile in Babylon. The Epistles are frequently chosen to match the Old Testament Lessons.

SEE PAGES 202–205 FOR OTHER SUGGESTED HYMNS

	FIRST LESSON	PSALM
Year C	**Deut. 26:(1–4)5–11**	**Psalm 91:9–15**
1 Lent	*The Israelite Confession of Faith*	or
(The Temptation of our Lord)	A wandering Aramean was my father; and he went down into Egypt. We cried to the Lord the God of our fathers . . . and the Lord brought us out of Egypt.	**Refrain:** He shall give his angels charge over you, to keep you in all your ways. *Psalm 91* 9,10/12,13/14,15
Hymn 61		
Year C	**Gen. 15:1–12,17–18**	**Psalm 27:10–18**
2 Lent	*The Covenant with Abraham*	or
Hymn 213 or 434	The Lord brought Abram outside and said, Look toward heaven and number the stars. So shall your descendents be. And he believed the Lord; and he reckoned it to him as righteousness.	**Refrain:** The Lord is my light and my salvation. *Psalm 27* 10,11/12,13/14,15/17,18

SECOND LESSON	CHANT BEFORE GOSPEL	GOSPEL
Romans 10:(5–8a)8b–13 If you confess with your lips that Jesus is Lord and believe in your heart that God raised him from the dead, you will be saved.	**Verse** (Matt. 4:4) Man shall not live by bread alone,* but by every word that proceeds from the mouth of God. *or* **Tract** Psalm 91:1–4(9–11)	**Luke 4:1–13** Jesus was led by the Spirit for forty days in the wilderness, tempted by the devil.
Phil. 3:17—4:1 Our commonwealth is in heaven, and from it we await a Savior, the Lord Jesus Christ.	**Verse** (Amos 5:14) Seek good, and not evil, that you may live;* and the God of hosts will be with you. *or* **Tract** Psalm 106:1–5 *(Omit the initial Hallelujah)*	**Luke 13:(22–30)31–35** O Jerusalem . . . killing the prophets. How often would I have gathered your children together as a hen gathers her brood under her wings. Behold, your house is forsaken.

	FIRST LESSON	PSALM

Year C	Exodus 3:1–15	Psalm 103:1–11
3 Lent	*The Burning Bush*	*or*
Hymn 522	God said to Moses, I AM WHO I AM. And he said, Say this to the people of Israel, I AM has sent me to you.	**Refrain:** The Lord is full of compassion and mercy, slow to anger and of great kindness. *Psalm 103* 1,2/3,4/6,7/10,11

Year C	Joshua (4:19–24); 5:9–12	Psalm 34:1–8
4 Lent	*First Passover in the Promised Land*	*or*
(The Communion Banquet)	While the people of Israel were . . . in Gilgal they kept the passover. After the passover . . . they ate of the produce of the land.	**Refrain:** Taste and see that the Lord is good. *Psalm 34* 1,2/3,4/5,6/7,8
Hymn 195 Entrance Hymn 597 Dismissal Hymn 584		

Year C	Isaiah 43:16–21	Psalm 126
5 Lent	*Prophecy of Deliverance*	*or*
Hymn 71	I give water in the wilderness . . . to give drink to my chosen people . . . whom I formed for myself that they might declare my praise.	**Refrain:** The Lord has done great things for us, and we are glad indeed. *Psalm 126* 1,2/3,4/5,6/7

SECOND LESSON	CHANT BEFORE GOSPEL	GOSPEL
1 Cor. 10:1–13	**Verse**	**Luke 13:1–9**
Our fathers . . . were baptized into Moses in the cloud and in the sea, and all ate the same supernatural food and all drank the same supernatural drink.	(2 Cor. 6:2) Behold, now is the acceptable time;* behold, now is the day of salvation. *or* **Tract** Psalm 42:1–7	A man had a fig tree . . . he came seeking fruit on it and found none. Lo, these three years I have come seeking fruit . . . and I find none. Cut it down.
2 Cor. 5:17–21	**Verse**	**Luke 15:11–32**
If any one is in Christ, he is a new creation; the old has passed away, behold the new has come.	(Luke 15:18) I will arise and go to my Father, and will say to him:* Father, I have sinned against heaven and before you. *or* **Tract** Psalm 122:(1–5)6–9	Let us eat and make merry; for this my son was dead and is alive again; he was lost and is found.
Philippians 3:8–14	**Verse**	**Luke 20:9–19**
For his sake I have suffered the loss of all things . . . in order that I may gain Christ and be found in him.	(Ps. 118:22,23) The stone which the builders rejected has become the chief cornerstone;* this is the Lord's doing, and it is marvelous in our eyes. *or* **Tract** Psalm 129:1–4(5–8)	A man planted a vineyard, and let it out to tenants. This is the heir; let us kill him, that the inheritance may be ours.

Liturgy of the Palms: Page 270. Gospel of the Palms:
Luke 19:29–40. At the Procession: Hymn 62 & Psalm 118:19–29.
Refrain after each verse of the Psalm: Hosanna in the highest.

	FIRST LESSON	PSALM
Year C	**Isaiah 45:21–25**	**Psalm 22:1–11**
The Sunday of The Passion	Turn to me and be saved. To me every knee shall bow.	*or* **Refrain:** My God, my God, why have you forsaken me?
or		*Psalm 22*
Palm Sunday	*or* **Isaiah 52:13—53:12**	1,2,3/4,5,6/7,8,9/10,11
Hymn 68 or 67	He has borne our griefs. He was wounded for our transgressions.	
Year ABC	**Isaiah 42:1–9**	**Psalm 36:5–10**
Monday in Holy Week	*First Song of the Servant of Yahweh*	*or*
Hymn 69	Behold my servant, whom I uphold, my chosen, in whom my soul delights: I have put my Spirit upon him, he will bring forth justice to the nations.	**Refrain:** In your light, O God, we see light. *Psalm 36* 5,6/7,8/9,10

SECOND LESSON	CHANT BEFORE GOSPEL	GOSPEL
Philippians 2:5–11	**Verse**	**Luke 22:39—23:49(50–56)** *or* **Luke 23:1–49(50–56)**
He humbled himself and became obedient unto death . . . that at the name of Jesus every knee should bow.	(Phil. 2:8,9) Christ for us became obedient unto death, even death on a cross;* therefore God has highly exalted him and bestowed on him the name which is above every name.	The Passion of Our Lord Jesus Christ.
	or **Tract** Psalm 22:26–30	
Hebrews 11:39—12:3	**Verse**	**John 12:1–11**
Looking to Jesus . . . who for the joy that was set before him endured the cross, despising the shame, and is seated at the right hand of the throne of God.	We adore you, O Christ, and we bless you,* because by your holy cross you have redeemed the world.	Six day before the Passover, Jesus came to Bethany. Mary took a pound of costly ointment . . . and anointed the feet of Jesus.
	or **Tract** Psalm 102:1–4,12–13	*or* **Mark 14:3–9** She has anointed my body beforehand for burying. And truly, I say to you . . . what she has done will be told in memory of her.

Year ABC	**Isaiah 49:1–6**	**Psalm 71:1–12**
Tuesday in Holy Week	*Second Song of the Servant of Yahweh*	*or* **Refrain:** I have taken refuge in you, O Lord. *Psalm 71* 2,3/4,10/11,12
Hymn 73	It is too light a thing that you should be my servant to raise up the tribes of Jacob and to restore the preserved of Israel; I will give you as a light to the nations, that my salvation may reach to the end of the earth.	

Year ABC	**Isaiah 50:4–9a**	**Psalm 69:7–15,22–23**
Wednesday in Holy Week	*Third Song of the Servant of Yahweh*	*or* **Refrain:** Answer me, O God, in your great mercy. *Psalm 69* 7,8/9,10/14,15/22,23
Hymn 81	I gave my back to the smiters, and my cheeks to those who pulled out the beard; I hid not my face from shame and spitting.	

Year ABC	**Exodus 12:1–14a**	**Psalm 78:14–20,23–25**
Maundy Thursday	This month shall be for you the beginning of months. They shall take every man a lamb . . . a lamb for a household. It is the Lord's passover.	*or* **Refrain:** Mortals ate the bread of angels, for the Lord gave them manna from heaven. *Psalm 78* 14,15/17,18/19,23/24,25
(The Lord's Supper)		
Hymn 195		

Proper Liturgy, page 274

SECOND LESSON	CHANT BEFORE GOSPEL	GOSPEL
1 Cor. 1:18–31 The word of the cross is folly to those who are perishing, but to us who are being saved it is the power of God.	**Verse or Tract** *As on Monday*	**John 12:37–38,42–50** Jesus said, He who believes in me, believes not in me but in him who sent me. *or* **Mark 11:15–19** Jesus entered the temple and began to drive out those who sold and those who bought. Is it not written, "My house shall be called a house of prayer for all the nations?"
Heb. 9:11–15,24–28 When Christ appeared as a high priest of the good things that have come . . . he entered once for all into the Holy Place, taking . . . his own blood, thus securing an eternal redemption.	**Verse or Tract** *As on Monday*	**John 13:21–35** Jesus testified, Truly, truly, I say to you, one of you will betray me. *or* **Matt. 26:1–5,14–25** Judas went to the chief priests and said, What will you give me if I deliver him to you?
1 Corinthians 11:23–26(27–32) This is my body. This cup is the new covenant in my blood. Do this in remembrance of me.	**Verse** (John 13:34) A new commandment I give to you:* love one another as I have loved you. *or* **Tract** Psalm 43	**John 13:1–15** Jesus began to wash the disciples' feet. *or* **Luke 22:14–30** Jesus took a cup, and . . . said, Take this, and divide it. He took bread, and broke it, saying, This is my body.

Hymns 199 and 200 may appropriately be sung after the postcommunion prayer.

	FIRST LESSON	PSALM
Year ABC	**Isaiah 52:13—53:12**	**Psalm 22:1–11**
Good Friday	*Fourth Song of the Servant of Yahweh*	*or* **Refrain:** My God, my
Hymn 75	He was wounded for our transgressions . . . He was numbered with the transgressors.	God, why have you forsaken me? *Psalm 22* 1,2/7,8/14,15/16,17/18, 19/20,21
	or **Genesis 22:1–18** You have not withheld your son, your only son.	
	or **Wisdom 2:1,12–24** If the righteous man is God's son, he will help him. Let us condemn him to a shameful death.	
Proper Liturgy, page 276		
Year ABC	**Job 14:1–14**	**Psalm 31:1–5**
Holy Saturday	If a man die, shall he live again?	*or* **Refrain** (Luke 23:46):
Hymn 83		Father, into your hands I commend my spirit. *Psalm 31* 1,2/3,4/5,16
Proper Liturgy, page 283		

SECOND LESSON	CHANT BEFORE GOSPEL	GOSPEL
Hebrews 10:1–25 "A body hast thou prepared for me." By a single offering he has perfected for all time those who are sanctified. There is no longer any offering for sin.	**Verse** (Phil. 2:8,9) Christ for us became obedient unto death, even death on a cross;* therefore God has highly exalted him and bestowed on him the name which is above every name. *or* **Tract** Psalm 40:1–14 *or* Psalm 69:1–10,14–23	**John (18:1–40);19:1–37** *The Passion of our Lord Jesus Christ* It is finished.
1 Peter 4:1–8 The Gentiles will give account to him who is ready to judge the living and the dead. This is why the gospel was preached even to the dead.	**Verse** We adore you, O Christ, and we bless you,* because by your holy cross you have redeemed the world. *or* **Tract** Psalm 130	**Matthew 27:57–66** *or* **John 19:38–42** *The Burial of our Lord Jesus Christ*

The Great Vigil of Easter: Liturgy of the Word.

At least two of the following Lessons are read, of which one is always the Lesson from Exodus. Four or five Lessons are customary. After each Lesson, the Psalm or Canticle listed, or some other suitable psalm, canticle, or hymn may be sung. A period of silence may be kept, and the Collect provided, or some other suitable Collect may be said. The entire Great Vigil of Easter may be found on pages 284-285 of the Prayer Book.

1. **Genesis 1:1—2:2**

   The Story of Creation

   Psalm 33:1–11
   or **Psalm 36:5–10**

   or
   Refrain: By the word of the Lord were the heavens made, by the breath of his mouth all the heavenly hosts.
   Psalm 33
   1,2/3,4/5,7/8,9/10,11

   or
   Refrain: In your light, O God, we see light.
   Psalm 36
   5,6/7,8/9,10

2. **Genesis 7:1–5,11–18; 8:6–18; 9:8–13**

   The Flood

   Psalm 46

   or
   Refrain: The Lord of hosts is with us; the God of Jacob is our stronghold.
   Psalm 46
   1,2,3/5,6,7/9,10,11

3. **Genesis 22:1–18**

   Abraham's sacrifice of Isaac

   Psalm 33:12–22
   or **Psalm 16**

   or
   Refrain: Happy is the nation whose God is the Lord.
   Psalm 33
   13,14,15/16,18,19/20,21,22

   or
   Refrain: Protect me, O God, for I take refuge in you.
   Psalm 16
   5,6/8,9/10,11

4. **Exodus 14:10—15:1**

   Israel's deliverance at the Red Sea

   Canticle 8, The Song of Moses

   or
   Refrain: I will sing to the Lord, for he has risen up in might.
   Canticle 8
   1,2/3,4/5,6/7,8/9,10/11,12,13

5. **Isaiah 4:2–6**

*God's Presence in a
Renewed Israel*

Psalm 122

or
Refrain: Pray for the peace of Jerusalem.
Psalm 122
1,2/3,4/6,7/8,9

6. **Isaiah 55:1–11**

*Salvation offered freely to
all*

Canticle 9, The First Song of Isaiah

or
Refrain: You shall draw water with rejoicing
from the springs of salvation.
Canticle 9
1,2/4,5/6,7

7. **Ezekiel 36:24–28**

*A new heart and a new
spirit*

Psalm 42:1–7

or
Refrain: As the deer longs for the water-brooks,
so longs my soul for you, O God.
Psalm 42
2,3/4,5/6,7

8. **Ezekiel 37:1–14**

The valley of dry bones

Psalm 30
or **Psalm 143**

or
Refrain: You brought me up, O Lord, from the
dead.
Psalm 30
1,2,3/4,5,6/12,13

or
Refrain: Revive me, O Lord, for your Name's
sake.
Psalm 143
1,2/4,5/6,7/8,10

9. **Zephaniah 3:12–20**

*The gathering of God's
people*

Psalm 98
or **Psalm 126**

or
Refrain: Shout with joy to the Lord, all you
lands; lift up your voice, rejoice, and sing.
Psalm 98
1,2/3,4/6,7/8,9

or
Refrain: The Lord has done great things for us,
and we are glad indeed.
Psalm 126
1,2/3,4/5,6/7

Year ABC

Easter Day

After the Collect of the Vigil Eucharist, continue with the Epistle.

At the Vigil or Early
Service

At an early Service, use one of the Old Testament Lessons from the Vigil followed by the corresponding Psalm or Canticle.

Year C	**Acts 10:34–43**	**Psalm** **118:14–17,22–24**
Easter Day	God raised him on the third day and made him manifest.	
Principal Service		*or*
Hymn 97		**Refrain:** On this day the Lord has acted; we will rejoice and be glad in it.
	or **Isaiah 51:9–11** Thou . . . didst make the depths of the sea a way for the redeemed to pass over.	*Psalm 118* 14,15/16,17/22,23

Year ABC	**Acts 5:29a,30–32**	**Psalm 114** *or* **Psalm 118:14–17, 22–24** *or* **Psalm 136**
Easter Day	The God of our fathers raised Jesus whom you killed by hanging him on a tree.	
Evening Service		*or*
Hymn 207		**Refrain:** Hallelujah! *Psalm 114* 1,2/3,4/5,6/7,8
	or **Daniel 12:1–3** Many of those who sleep in the dust of the earth shall awake, some to everlasting life, and some to shame and everlasting contempt.	*or Psalm 118 as at the principal service*

SECOND LESSON	ALLELUIA	GOSPEL
Romans 6:3–11	**Alleluia**	**Matthew 28:1–10**
All of us who have been baptized into Christ Jesus were baptized into his death . . . so that as Christ was raised . . . we too might walk in newness of life.	V. Alleluia. R. Alleluia. *Repeated three times, followed by:* **Refrain:** Hallelujah! *Psalm 114* 1,2/3,4/5,6/7,8 *If preferred, the Psalm may be sung without Refrain.*	After the sabbath, toward the dawn of the first day of the week . . . He is not here; for he has risen. *Offertory Hymn:* 89
Colossians 3:1–4	**Alleluia**	**Luke 24:1–10**
You have been raised with Christ. For you have died, and your life is hid with Christ in God. *or* **Acts 10:34–43**	(1 Cor. 5:7,8) Christ our Passover is sacrificed for us:* therefore let us keep the feast.	Why do you seek the living among the dead? He is not here, but has risen.
1 Cor. 5:6b–8	**Alleluia**	**Luke 24:13–35**
Christ, our paschal lamb, has been sacrificed. Let us, therefore, celebrate the festival, not with the old leaven, the leaven of malice and evil, but with the unleavened bread of sincerity and truth. *or* **Acts 5:29a,30–32**	*As at the Morning Service*	That very day two of them were going to a village named Emmaus . . . When he was at table with them, he took the bread and blessed, and broke it, and gave it to them. And their eyes were opened and they recognized him.

	FIRST LESSON	PSALM
Year ABC Monday in Easter Week Hymn 91	Acts 2:14,22b–32 Peter addressed them. This Jesus, delivered up according to the definite plan and foreknowledge of God, you crucified and killed by the hands of lawless men. But God raised him up. Of that we all are witnesses.	— Psalm 16:8–11 or Psalm 118:19–24 or **Refrain:** Hallelujah! *Psalm 16* 8/9/10/11 or **Refrain:** Give thanks to the Lord, for he is good, his mercy endures for ever. or Hallelujah! *Psalm 118* 19,20/21,22/23,24
Year ABC Tuesday in Easter Week Hymn 100 (tune 113)	Acts 2:36–41 Let all the house of Israel therefore know assuredly that God has made him both Lord and Christ. Repent, and be baptized.	Psalm 33:18–22 or **Refrain:** Hallelujah! *Psalm 33* 1,2/18,19/20,21 *or Psalm 118 as on Monday*
Year ABC Wednesday in Easter Week Hymn 207	Acts 3:1–10 Peter said, I have no silver and gold, but I give you what I have; in the name of Jesus Christ of Nazareth, walk.	Psalm 105:1–8 or **Refrain:** Hallelujah! *Psalm 105* 1,2/3,4/5,6/7,8 *or Psalm 118 as on Monday*

	Alleluia	Matthew 28:9-15
In place of the Psalm, an Alleluia Verse may be used.	(Psalm 118:24) On this day the Lord has acted;* we will rejoice and be glad in it.	When the chief priests had assembled with the elders and taken counsel, they gave a sum of money to the soldiers and said, Tell people, "His disciples came by night and stole him away while we were asleep."
	Alleluia	John 20:11-18
	As on Monday	Mary Magdelene saw Jesus standing, but she did not know that it was Jesus. Supposing him to be the gardener, she said to him, Sir, if you have carried him away, tell me where. Jesus said to her, Mary. She turned and said to him in Hebrew, Rabboni!
	Alleluia	Luke 24:13-35
	As on Monday	Two of the disciples were going to . . . Emmaus. When he was at table with them, he took the bread and blessed, and broke it, and gave it to them. Their eyes were opened and they recognized him.

HYMNS	FIRST LESSON	PSALM
Year ABC Thursday in Easter Week Hymn 94	**Acts 3:11–26** Peter addressed the people. You denied the Holy and Righteous One, and asked for a murderer to be granted to you, and killed the Author of life, whom God raised from the dead.	**Psalm 8** or **Psalm 114** or **Refrain:** Hallelujah! *Psalm 8* 1,2/4,5/6,7 or **Refrain:** Hallelujah! *Psalm 114* 1,2/3,4/5,6/7,8 or *Psalm 118 as on Monday*
Year ABC Friday in Easter Week Hymn 437 (tune 391)	**Acts 4:1–12** The priests and the captain of the temple and the Sadducees arrested them. Peter, filled with the Holy Spirit, said, Rulers . . . be it known to you all . . . that by the name of Jesus Christ . . . this man is standing before you well.	**Psalm 116:1–8** or **Refrain:** Hallelujah! *Psalm 116* 1/2,3/5,6/7,8 or *Psalm 118 as on Monday*
Year ABC Saturday in Easter Week Hymn 98	**Acts 4:13–21** They saw the boldness of Peter and John . . . and charged them not to speak. Peter and John answered them . . . We cannot but speak of what we have seen and heard.	**Psalm 118:14–18** or **Refrain:** Hallelujah! *Psalm 118* 1,14/15,16/17,18 or *Psalm 118 as on Monday*

	ALLELUIA	GOSPEL
In place of the Psalm, an Alleluia Verse may be used.	**Alleluia** *As on Monday*	**Luke 24:36b–48** Jesus himself stood among them. But they were startled and frightened, and supposed that they saw a spirit. See my hands and my feet, that it is I myself; handle me and see. Then he opened their minds to understand the scriptures.
	Alleluia *As on Monday*	**John 21:1–14** Jesus revealed himself again to the disciples by the Sea of Tiberias. He said, Cast the net on the right side of the boat. Peter . . . hauled the net ashore, full of large fish, a hundred and fifty-three of them.
	Alleluia *As on Monday*	**Mark 16:9–15,20** When Jesus rose early on the first day of the week, he appeared to Mary Magdelene. Afterward he appeared to the eleven. He upbraided them for their unbelief and hardness of heart, because they had not believed those who saw him. Go into all the world and preach the gospel.

In Easter Season a Reading from the Acts of the Apostles normally takes the place of an Old Testament Lesson.

SEE PAGES 202–205 FOR OTHER SUGGESTED HYMNS

	FIRST LESSON	PSALM
Year C 2 of Easter (The Sunday of Thomas) Hymn 99	**Acts 5:12a,17–22,25–29** The Sadducees arrested the apostles and put them in . . . prison. An angel . . . opened the prison . . . and said, Go and stand in the temple and speak. *or* **Job 42:1–6** I had heard of thee by the hearing of the ear, but now my eye sees thee.	**Psalm 118:19–24** *or* **Psalm 111** *or* **Refrain:** Give thanks to the Lord, for he is good; his mercy endures for ever. *or* Hallelujah! *Psalm 118* 19,20/21,22/23,24 *or* **Refrain:** Hallelujah! *Psalm 111* 1,2/3,4/9,10
Year C 3 of Easter Hymn 207	**Acts 9:1–19a** Saul, Saul, why do you persecute me? Saul said, Who are you, Lord? I am Jesus, whom you are persecuting. *or* **Jer. 32:36–41** I will make with them an everlasting covenant.	**Psalm 33:1–11** *or* **Refrain** (Ps. 98:1): Sing to the Lord a new song. *or* Hallelujah! *Psalm 33* 1,3/4,5/10,11

The Gospels for the first three Sundays of Easter present the principal resurrection narratives. Good Shepherd Sunday is now the fourth Sunday of the season. The rest of the Sundays of Easter take their Gospels from the Johannine discourses.

SECOND LESSON	ALLELUIA	GOSPEL
Rev. 1:(1–8)9–19	**Alleluia**	**John 20:19–31**
I am the first and the last, and the living one; I died, and behold I am alive for evermore. *or* **Acts 5:12a,17–22, 25–29**	(John 20:29) You believe in me, Thomas, because you have seen me;* blessed are those who have not seen and yet believe.	The first day of the week . . . Receive the Holy Spirit . . . Eight days later . . . Blessed are those who have not seen and yet believe.
Revelation 5:6–14	**Alleluia**	**John 21:1–14**
Worthy art thou . . . for thou . . . didst ransom men . . . made them a kingdom and priests to our God. *or* **Acts 9:1–19a**	(Rom. 6:9) Christ being raised from the dead will never die again;* death no longer has dominion over him.	Simon Peter . . . hauled the net ashore, full of large fish . . . Jesus said . . . Come and have breakfast . . . This was now the third time that Jesus was revealed . . . after he was raised from the dead.

	FIRST LESSON	PSALM

Year C

4 of Easter

(The Good Shepherd)

Hymn 345

**Acts
13:15–16,26–33(34–39)**

We bring you the good news that what God promised . . . he has fulfilled . . . by raising Jesus.

or **Numbers 27:12–23**
That the congregation . . . may not be as sheep which have no shepherd.

Psalm 100

or
Refrain: We are his people and the sheep of his pasture.
or Hallelujah!
Psalm 100
1/2/3/4

Year C

5 of Easter

Hymn 479

Acts 13:44–52

I have set you to be a light for the Gentiles, that you may bring salvation to the uttermost parts of the earth.

or **Lev. 19:1–2,9–18**
Say to . . . the people of Israel, You shall be holy; for I the Lord your God am holy.

Psalm 145:1–9

or
Refrain: I will exalt you, O God my King, and bless your Name for ever and ever.
or Hallelujah!
Psalm 145
3,4/5,6/8,9

Year C

6 of Easter

Hymn 378
Entrance Hymn 474

Acts 14:8–18

Paul said, God did good and gave you from heaven rains and fruitful seasons.

or **Joel 2:21–27**
Beasts of the field . . . fig tree and vine give their full yield. Vats shall overflow with wine and oil.

Psalm 67

or
Refrain: Let the peoples praise you, O God; let all the peoples praise you.
Psalm 67
1,2/4/6,7

or Hallelujah!
Psalm 67
1,2/3,4/6,7

Revelation 7:9–17	**Alleluia**	**John 10:22–30**
The Lamb in the midst of the throne will be their shepherd, and he will guide them to springs of living water.	(John 10:14) I am the good shepherd, says the Lord;* I know my sheep, and my sheep know me.	My sheep hear my voice and I know them, and they follow me; and I give them eternal life.
or **Acts 13:15–16,26–33(34–39)**		

Rev. 19:1,4–9	**Alleluia**	**John 13:31–35**
Let us rejoice and exult and give him the glory, for the marriage of the Lamb has come, and his bride has made herself ready.	(John 13:34) A new commandment I give to you:* love one another as I have loved you.	Now is the Son of man glorified. Love one another; even as I have loved you. By this all men will know that you are my disciples.
or **Acts 13:44–52**		

Rev. 21:22—22:5	**Alleluia**	**John 14:23–29**
The angel showed me . . . the tree of life with its twelve kinds of fruit, yielding its fruit each month.	(John 14:23) If anyone loves me, he will keep my word;* and my Father will love him, and we will come to him.	The Counselor, the Holy Spirit, whom the Father will send in my name, he will teach you all things, and bring to your remembrance all that I have said to you.
or **Acts 14:8–18**		

	FIRST LESSON	PSALM
Year C Ascension Day Hymn 104	**Acts 1:1–11** Men of Galilee, why do you stand looking into heaven? *or* **2 Kings 2:1–15** Elijah went up by a whirlwind into heaven. Elisha saw it and he cried, My father, my father!	**Psalm 110:1–5** *or* **Psalm 47** *or* **Refrain** (Matt. 28:20): I am with you always, to the close of the age. *or* Hallelujah! *Psalm 110* 1/2/3/4 *or* **Refrain:** God has gone up with a shout, the Lord with the sound of the ram's-horn. *or* Hallelujah! *Psalm 47* 1,2/5,6/7,8
Year C 7 of Easter Hymn 356	**Acts 16:16–34** There was a great earthquake . . . all the doors were opened and every one's fetters were unfastened. The jailer was baptized at once, with his family. *or* **1 Sam. 12:19–24** The people said to Samuel, Pray for your servants to the Lord.	**Psalm 47** *or* **Psalm 68:1–20** *or* **Refrain:** God has gone up with a shout, the Lord with the sound of the ram's-horn. *or* Hallelujah! *Psalm 47* 1,2/5,6/7,8 *or* **Refrain:** Sing to God O kingdoms of the earth; sing praises to the Lord. *or* Hallelujah! *Psalm 68* 4,5/7,8/17,18

SECOND LESSON	ALLELUIA	GOSPEL
Ephesians 1:15–23	**Alleluia**	**Luke 24:49–53**
The riches of his glorious inheritance in the saints . . . which he accomplished in Christ when he raised him from the dead. *or* **Acts 1:1–11**	(Matt. 28:19,20) Go and make disciples of all nations;* I am with you always, to the close of the age.	While he blessed them, he parted from them, and was carried up into heaven. *or* **Mark 16:9–15,19–20** The Lord Jesus . . . was taken up into heaven, and sat down at the right hand of God.
Revelation 22:12–14,16–17,20	**Alleluia**	**John 17:20–26**
Let him who is thirsty come, let him who desires take the water of life without price. *or* **Acts 16:16–34**	(John 14:18) The Lord said, I will not leave you desolate;* I will come back to you, and your hearts will rejoice.	Jesus said, I do not pray for these only, but also for those who believe in me through their word, that they may all be one.

	FIRST LESSON	PSALM
Year ABC	**Genesis 11:1–9**	**Psalm 33:12–22**
Vigil of Pentecost	*The Tower of Babel*	*or*
or		**Refrain:** Happy is the nation whose God is the Lord.
Early Service		*Psalm 33* 13,14,15/16,18,19/20,21,22
	Exodus 19:1–9,16–20a,20:18–20	**Canticle 2 or 13**
		or
	The Covenant	**Refrain** (Exod. 19:6): He has made us a kingdom of priests and a holy nation. *Canticle 13* 1,2/3,4/5,6
	Ezekiel 37:1–14	**Psalm 130**
	The valley of dry bones	*or* **Refrain:** With the Lord there is mercy; with him there is Plenteous redemption. *Psalm 130* 1/2,3/4,5/6,7
	Joel 2:28–32	**Canticle 9**
	God will pour out his Spirit.	*or* **Refrain:** You shall draw water with rejoicing from the springs of salvation. *Canticle 9* 1,2/4,5/6,7
	Acts 2:1–11	**Psalm 104:25–32**
	The Story of Pentecost	*or* **Refrain:** Send forth your Spirit, O Lord, and renew the face of the earth. *or* Hallelujah! *Psalm 104* 25,26/28,29/30,31/32,35

SECOND LESSON	ALLELUIA	GOSPEL
Romans 8:14–17,22–27	**Alleluia**	**John 7:37–39a**
All who are led by the Spirit of God are sons of God. *or* **Acts 2:1–11**	Come, Holy Spirit, and fill the hearts of your faithful people,* and kindle in them the fire of your love.	If any one thirst, let him come to me and drink. This he said about the Spirit.

It is appropriate that the Gospel be read several times, each time in a different language.

	FIRST LESSON	PSALM
Year C The Day of Pentecost Principal Service Hymn 109	**Acts 2:1–11** When the day of Pentecost had come, they were all together in one place. or **Joel 2:28–32** I will pour out my spirit on all flesh; your sons and your daughters shall prophesy.	**Psalm 104:25–32** or **Psalm 33:12–15,18–22** or **Refrain:** Send forth your Spirit, O Lord, and renew the face of the earth. or Hallelujah! *Psalm 104* 25,26/28,29/30,31/32,35
Year C Trinity Sunday Hymn 266	**Isaiah 6:1–8** In the year that King Uzziah died I saw the Lord. "Holy, holy, holy is the Lord of host; the whole earth is full of his glory." Then I said, Here am I! Send me.	**Canticle 2 or 13** or **Psalm 29** or **Refrain:** Glory to you, Father, Son, and Holy Spirit. *Canticle 13* 1,2/3,4/5,6 or **Refrain:** Ascribe to the Lord the glory due his Name. *Psalm 29* 3,4,5/6,7,8/9,10,11

1 Cor. 12:4–13	**Alleluia**	**John 20:19–23**
To each is given the manifestation of the Spirit for the common good.	Come, Holy Spirit, and fill the hearts of your faithful people,* and kindle in them the fire of your love.	Receive the Holy Spirit. If you forgive the sins of any, they are forgiven.
or **Acts 2:1–11**		*or* **John 14:8–17** If you love me, you will keep my commandments. And I will pray the Father, and he will give you another Counselor, to be with you for ever.
Rev. 4:1–11	**Alleluia**	**John 16:(5–11)12–15**
At once I was in the Spirit, and lo, a throne stood in heaven, with one seated on the throne. "Holy, holy, holy, is the Lord God Almighty, who was and is and is to come!"	(Rev. 1:4) Glory to the Father and to the Son and to the Holy Spirit:* to God who is, and who was, and who is to come.	When the Spirit of truth comes, he will guide you into all the truth; for he will not speak on his own authority, but whatever he hears he will speak and he will declare to you the things that are to come.

The Gospels for the Sundays after Pentecost in Year C continue the reading of the Gospel according to Luke begun on the Sundays after Epiphany. The Second Lessons consist of semi-continuous readings from the Epistles. The Old Testament Lessons are chosen to match the Gospel (or, occasionally, the Epistle).

SEE PAGES 202–205 FOR OTHER SUGGESTED HYMNS

	FIRST LESSON	PSALM
Year C Proper 1 Closest to May 11 Hymn 418	**Jeremiah 17:5–10** Cursed is the man who trusts in man. Blessed is the man who trusts in the Lord.	**Psalm 1** *or* **Refrain:** Happy are they whose delight is in the law of the Lord. *Psalm 1* 1,2/3,4/5,6
Year C Proper 2 Closest to May 18 Hymn 298	**Gen. 45:3–11,21–28** Joseph said to his brothers, Come near to me, I pray you. Do not be distressed, or angry with yourselves. God sent me before you to preserve a remnant on earth. It was not you who sent me here, but God.	**Psalm 37:3–10** *or* **Refrain:** Put your trust in the Lord and do good. *Psalm 37* 1,3/4,5/6,7/8,10
Year C Proper 3 Closest to May 25 Hymn 564	**Jeremiah 7:1–7(8–15)** Do not trust in these deceptive words: This is the temple of the Lord. For if you truly amend your ways . . . and . . . execute justice . . . then I will let you dwell in this place.	**Psalm 92:1–5,11–14** *or* **Refrain:** It is a good thing to give thanks to the Lord. *Psalm 92* 2,3/11,12/13,14

SECOND LESSON	ALLELUIA	GOSPEL
1 Cor. 15:12–20	**Alleluia**	**Luke 6:17–26**
How can some of you say that there is no resurrection of the dead? Christ has been raised from the dead.	*Ad libitum* *(See page 206)*	Blessed are you poor, for yours is the kingdom of God. Woe to you that are rich.
1 Cor. 15:35–38,42–50	**Alleluia**	**Luke 6:27–38**
Just as we have borne the image of the man of dust, we shall also bear the image of the man of heaven.	*Ad libitum*	Love your enemies . . . Do not withhold your coat. Judge not, and you will not be judged . . . forgive, and you will be forgiven.
1 Cor. 15:50–58	**Alleluia**	**Luke 6:39–49**
The sting of death is sin, and the power of sin is the law. But thanks be to God who gives us the victory through our Lord Jesus Christ.	*Ad libitum*	Why do you call me "Lord, Lord," and not do what I tell you?

	FIRST LESSON	PSALM
Year C Proper 4 Closest to June 1 Hymn 263	**1 Kings** **8:22–23,27–30,41–43** When a foreigner . . . comes and prays . . . hear thou in heaven thy dwelling place, and do according to all for which the foreigner calls to thee.	Psalm 96:1–9 *or* **Refrain:** Sing to the Lord a new song, sing to the Lord, all the whole earth. *Psalm 96* 2,3/4,5/6,7/8,9
Year C Proper 5 Closest to June 8 Hymn 453 or 515	**1 Kings 17:17–24** The son of the woman . . . became ill. The Lord hearkened to the voice Elijah . . . the soul of the child came into him again.	Psalm 30:1–6,12–13 *or* **Refrain:** O Lord my God, I cried out to you, and you restored me to health. *Psalm 30* 1,3/4,5,6/12,13
Year C Proper 6 Closest to June 15 Hymn 284 or 69	**2 Samuel** **11:26—12:10,13–15** Nathan said to David . . . You have smitten Uriah the Hittite . . . and taken his wife. David said . . . I have sinned. Nathan said . . . The Lord also has put away your sin.	Psalm 32:1–8 *or* **Refrain:** I acknowledged my sin to you, and you forgave me the guilt of my sin. *Psalm 32* 1,2/3,4/5,6/7,8
Year C Proper 7 Closest to June 22 Hymn 71 or 344	**Zechariah 12:8–10;** **13:1** When they look on him whom they have pierced, they shall mourn for him, as one mourns for an only child, and weep bitterly over him, as one weeps over a first-born.	Psalm 63:1–8 *or* **Refrain:** Lord, my soul clings to you; your right hand holds me fast. *Psalm 63* 1,2/3,4/5,7

SECOND LESSON	ALLELUIA	GOSPEL
Galatians 1:1–10	**Alleluia**	**Luke 7:1–10**
Even if we, or an angel from heaven, should preach to you a gospel contrary to that which we preached to you, let him be accursed.	*Ad libitum*	Now a centurion has a slave . . . who was sick. He loves our nation. Lord I am not worthy.
Galatians 1:11–24	**Alleluia**	**Luke 7:11–17**
The gospel which was preached by me is not man's gospel.	*Ad libitum*	A man who had died was being carried out, the only son of his mother, and she was a widow. Young man, I say to you, arise. The dead man began to speak.
Galatians 2:11–21	**Alleluia**	**Luke 7:36–50**
A man is not justified by works of the law but through faith in Jesus Christ	*Ad libitum*	A woman of the city, who was a sinner . . . began to wet his feet with her tears . . . and anointed them. Your sins are forgiven. Your faith has saved you; go in peace.
Galatians 3:23–29	**Alleluia**	**Luke 9:18–24**
There is neither Jew nor Greek, there is neither slave nor free, there is neither male nor female; for you are all one in Christ Jesus.	*Ad libitum*	The Son of man must suffer many things and be rejected by the elders . . . and be killed and on the third day be raised.

	FIRST LESSON	PSALM
Year C Proper 8 Closest to June 29 Hymn 220 or 573	**1 Kings 19:15–16,19–21** The Lord said to Elijah, Elisha . . . you shall anoint to be prophet in your place. Elijah passed by him and cast his mantle upon him. And he left the oxen, and ran after Elijah.	**Psalm 16:5–11** *or* **Refrain:** The Lord will show me the path of life. *Psalm 16* 5,6/7,8/9,10/11
Year C Proper 9 Closest to July 6 Hymn 575 or 576	**Isaiah 66:10–16** It shall be known that the hand of the Lord is with his servants, and his indignation is against his enemies.	**Psalm 66:1–8** *or* **Refrain:** Be joyful in God, all you lands. *Psalm 66* 1,2/3,4/5,6/7,8
Year C Proper 10 Closest to July 13 Hymn 493	**Deut. 30:9–14** Obey the voice of the Lord your God, to keep his commandments. Turn to the Lord your God with all your heart and with all your soul.	**Psalm 25:3–9** *or* **Refrain:** Lead me in your truth and teach me, for you are the God of my salvation. *Psalm 25* 3,5/6,7/8,9

SECOND LESSON	ALLELUIA	GOSPEL
Gal. 5:1,13–25 You were called to freedom . . . do not use your freedom as an opportunity for the flesh, but through love be servants of one another.	**Alleluia** *Ad libitum*	**Luke 9:51–62** Jesus said, Follow me. No one who puts his hand to the plow and looks back is fit for the kingdom of God.
Gal. 6:(1–10)14–18 Far be it from me to glory except in the cross of our Lord Jesus Christ.	**Alleluia** *Ad libitum*	**Luke 10:1–12,16–20** Jesus said, He who hears you hears me, and he who rejects you rejects me, and he who rejects me rejects him who sent me. I have given you authority to tread . . . over all the power of the enemy.
Colossians 1:1–14 We have not ceased to pray for you, asking that you may be filled with the knowledge of his will . . . to lead a life worthy of the Lord.	**Alleluia** *Ad libitum*	**Luke 10:25–37** Teacher, what shall I do to inherit eternal life? You shall love the Lord your God with all your heart, and with all your soul.

	FIRST LESSON	PSALM
Year C Proper 11 Closest to July 20 Hymn 477	**Genesis 18:1–10a(10b–14)** The Lord appeared to Abraham. Rest yourselves . . . while I fetch a morsel of bread. Abraham hastened to Sarah . . . make three cakes . . . ran to the herd, and took a calf . . . and set it before them. Where is Sarah . . . ? Your wife shall have a son.	**Psalm 15** *or* **Refrain:** The right righteous shall abide upon God's holy hill. *Psalm 15* 1,2/3,4/5,6/7
Year C Proper 12 Closest to July 27 Hymn 500 or 391	**Genesis 18:20–33** The outcry against Sodom and Gomorrah is great. Wilt thou destroy the righteous with the wicked? For the sake of ten I will not destroy it.	**Psalm 138** *or* **Refrain:** When I called, you answered me; O Lord, your love endures for ever. *Psalm 138* 1,2/3,4/7,8/9
Year C Proper 13 Closest to August 3 Hymn 501	**Ecclesiastes 1:12–14;2:(1–7,11)18–23** All is vanity and a striving after wind. I hated all my toil . . . seeing that I must leave it to the man who will come after me; and who knows whether he will be a wise man or a fool?	**Psalm 49:1–11** *or* **Refrain:** We can never ransom ourselves, or deliver to God the price of our life. *Psalm 49* 1,2/4,5/7,8/9,11

SECOND LESSON	ALLELUIA	GOSPEL
Colossians 1:21–29 You who once were estranged and hostile in mind . . . he has now reconciled in his body . . . to present you holy and blameless.	**Alleluia** *Ad libitum*	**Luke 10:38–42** Martha received him into her house. She had a sister called Mary, who sat at the Lord's feet and listened. Martha was distracted with much serving. Mary has chosen the good portion.
Colossians 2:6–15 As therefore you received Christ Jesus the Lord, so live in him, rooted and built up in him and established in the faith, just as you were taught, abounding in thanksgiving.	**Alleluia** *Ad libitum*	**Luke 11:1–13** When you pray, say: Father, hallowed be thy name. Ask and it will be given you.
Col. 3:(5–11)12–17 Put on love, which binds everything together in perfect harmony. Let the peace of Christ rule in your hearts.	**Alleluia** *Ad libitum*	**Luke 12:13–21** A man's life does not consist in the abundance of his possessions. Fool! This night your soul is required of you; and the things you have prepared, whose will they be?

	FIRST LESSON	PSALM

	FIRST LESSON	PSALM
Year C Proper 14 Closest to August 10 Hymn 285	**Genesis 15:1–6** Look toward heaven and number the stars. So shall your descendants be. He believed the Lord; and he reckoned it to him as righteousness.	**Psalm 33:12–15,18–22** *or* **Refrain:** Our soul waits for the Lord; he is our help and our shield. *Psalm 33* 13,14/18,19/21,22
Year C Proper 15 Closest to August 17 Hymn 312	**Jeremiah 23:23–29** Can a man hide himself in secret places so that I cannot see him? Is not my word like fire?	**Psalm 82** *or* **Refrain:** Arise, O God, and rule the earth, for you shall take all nations for your own. *Psalm 82* 1,2/4,5/6,7
Year C Proper 16 Closest to August 24 Hymn 534 or 543	**Isaiah 28:14–22** Behold I am laying in Zion for a foundation a stone, a tested stone, a precious cornerstone. He who believes will not be in haste.	**Psalm 46** *or* **Refrain:** The Lord of hosts is with us; the God of Jacob is our stronghold. *Psalm 46* 1,2,3/5,6,7/9,10,11
Year C Proper 17 Closest to August 31 Hymn 491 or 284	**Ecclesiastes 10:(7–11)12–18** The beginning of man's pride is to depart from the Lord. The Lord has cast down the thrones of rulers, and has seated the lowly in their place.	**Psalm 112** *or* **Refrain:** Happy are they who fear the Lord. *Psalm 112* 2,3/4,5/6,7/9

SECOND LESSON	ALLELUIA	GOSPEL
Hebrews **11:1–3(4–7)8–16** Faith is the assurance of things hoped for. By faith Sarah herself received power to conceive. Therefore . . . were born descendants as many as the stars of heaven.	**Alleluia** *Ad libitum*	**Luke 12:32–40** It is your Father's good pleasure to give you the kingdom. Blessed are those servants whom the master finds awake when he comes.
Hebrews **12:1–7(8–10)11–14** Since we are surrounded by so great a cloud of witnesses . . . let us run . . . the race that is set before us.	**Alleluia** *Ad libitum*	**Luke 12:49–56** I came to cast fire upon the earth. Do you think that I have come to give peace on earth? No . . . rather division.
Hebrews **12:18–19,22–29** Let us be grateful for receiving a kingdom that cannot be shaken, and thus let us offer to God acceptable worship, with reverence and awe.	**Alleluia** *Ad libitum*	**Luke 13:22–30** Will those who are saved be few? Strive to enter by the narrow door. Men will come from east and west . . . and sit at table in the kingdom of God.
Hebrews 13:1–8 Do not neglect to show hospitality to strangers, for thereby some have entertained angels unawares.	**Alleluia** *Ad libitum*	**Luke 14:1,7–14** When you are invited . . . to a marriage feast . . . do not sit down in a place of honor. When you give a dinner . . . invite the poor . . . you will be blest.

	FIRST LESSON	PSALM
Year C Proper 18 Closest to Sept. 7 Hymn 456 or 563	**Deut. 30:15–20** See I have set before you this day life and good, death and evil. Choose life, that you and your descendants may live, loving the Lord your God.	**Psalm 1** *or* **Refrain:** Happy are they whose delight is in the law of the Lord. *Psalm 1* 1,2/3,4/5,6
Year C Proper 19 Closest to Sept. 14 Hymn 518	**Exodus 32:1,7–14** The Lord said to Moses . . . Your people . . . have corrupted themselves. Moses besought the Lord . . . Remember Abraham, Isaac, and Israel.	**Psalm 51:1–11** *or* **Refrain:** Create in me a clean heart, O God. *Psalm 51* 1,2/3,4/7,8
Year C Proper 20 Closest to Sept. 21 Hymn 494	**Amos 8:4–7(8–12)** Hear this, you who trample on the needy. The Lord has sworn by the pride of Jacob: Surely I will never forget their deeds.	**Psalm 138** *or* **Refrain:** Give thanks to the Lord who cares for the lowly. *Psalm 138* 1,2/4,7/8,9
Year C Proper 21 Closest to Sept. 28 Hymn 301 or 560	**Amos 6:1–7** Woe to those who are at ease in Zion. They shall now be the first of those to go into exile.	**Psalm 146:4–9** *or* **Refrain:** Praise the Lord, O my soul. *Psalm 146* 4,5/6,7/8,9

SECOND LESSON	ALLELUIA	GOSPEL
Philemon 1–20	**Alleluia**	**Luke 14:25–33**
I appeal to you for my child Onesimus whose father I have become in my imprisonment. I am sending him back to you, sending my own heart.	*Ad libitum*	Whoever does not bear his own cross and come after me, cannot be my disciple. Whoever of you does not renounce all that he has cannot be my disciple.
1 Timothy 1:12–17	**Alleluia**	**Luke 15:1–10**
The saying is sure and worthy of full accpetance, that Christ Jesus came into the world to save sinners.	*Ad libitum*	There will be more joy in heaven over one sinner who repents than over ninety-nine righteous persons who need no repentance.
1 Timothy 2:1–8	**Alleluia**	**Luke 16:1–13**
I urge that . . . prayers, intercessions, and thanksgivings be made for all men.	*Ad libitum*	No servant can serve two masters. You cannot serve God and mammon.
1 Timothy 6:11–19	**Alleluia**	**Luke 16:19–31**
Fight the good fight of the faith. Keep the commandment unstained and free from reproach until the appearing of our Lord Jesus Christ . . . who alone has immortality and dwells in unapproachable light.	*Ad libitum*	The rich man called out, Father Abraham. Abraham said, They have Moses and the prophets; let them hear them.

	FIRST LESSON	PSALM
Year C Proper 22 Closest to Oct. 5 Hymn 572 or 431	**Habakkuk 1:1–6(7–11)12–13; 2:1–4** He whose soul is not upright in him shall fail . . . the righteous shall live by his faith.	**Psalm 37:3–10** *or* **Refrain:** Put your trust in the Lord and do good. *Psalm 37* 1,3/4,5/6,7/8,10
Year C Proper 23 Closest to Oct. 12 Hymn 517	**Ruth 1:(1–7)8–19a** Entreat me not to leave you . . . for where you go I will go . . . your people shall be my people, and your God my God.	**Psalm 113** *or* **Refrain:** Let the Name of the Lord be praised, from this time forth for evermore. *Psalm 113* 1,4/5,6/7,8
Year C Proper 24 Closest to Oct. 19 Hymn 314	**Gen. 32:3–8,22–30** Jacob was left alone; and a man wrestled with him. Your name shall no more be called Jacob, but Israel.	**Psalm 121** *or* **Refrain:** My help comes from the Lord, the maker of heaven and earth. *Psalm 121* 1,2/3,4/5,6/7,8
Year C Proper 25 Closest to Oct. 26 Hymn 417 or 560	**Jeremiah 14:(1–6)7–10,19–22** We acknowledge our wickedness, O Lord . . . for we have sinned against thee. Do not spurn us . . . and do not break thy covenant with us.	**Psalm 84:1–6** *or* **Refrain:** O Lord of hosts, happy are they who put their trust in you. *Psalm 84* 1,2/3,4/5,6

2 Tim. 1:(1–5)6–14 God did not give us a spirit of timidity but a spirit of power and love and self-control.	**Alleluia** *Ad libitum*	**Luke 17:5–10** If you had faith as a grain of mustard seed, you could say to this sycamore tree, Be rooted up, and be planted in the sea, and it would obey you.
2 Tim. 2:(3–7)8–15 If we have died with him, we shall also live with him. If we deny him, he also will deny us; if we are faithless, he remains faithful—for he cannot deny himself.	**Alleluia** *Ad libitum*	**Luke 17:11–19** Were not ten cleansed? Where are the nine? Was no one found to return and give praise to God except this foreigner?
2 Tim. 3:14—4:5 All scripture is inspired by God and profitable for teaching, for reproof, for correction, and for training in righteousness.	**Alleluia** *Ad libitum*	**Luke 18:1–8a** Will not God vindicate his elect, who cry to him day and night? He will vindicate them speedily.
2 Tim. 4:6–8,16–18 I have fought the good fight. Henceforth there is laid up for me the crown of righteousness.	**Alleluia** *Ad libitum*	**Luke 18:9–14** Two men went up into the temple to pray, one a Pharisee and the other a tax collector. Everyone who exalts himself will be humbled, but he who humbles himself will be exalted.

	FIRST LESSON	PSALM
Year C Proper 26 Closest to Nov. 2 Hymn 414	**Isaiah 1:10–20** Cease to do evil, learn to do good; seek justice, correct oppression. If you are willing and obedient, you shall eat the good of the land.	**Psalm 32:1–8** *or* **Refrain:** I acknowledged my sin to you, and you forgave me the guilt of my sin. *Psalm 32* 1,2/3,4/5,6/7,8
Year C Proper 27 Closest to Nov. 9 Hymn 225	**Job 19:23–27a** I know that my redeemer lives.	**Psalm 17:1–8** *or* **Refrain:** Keep me as the apple of your eye; hide me under the shadow of your wings. *Psalm 17* 1,2/3,5/6,7
Year C Proper 28 Closest to Nov. 16 Hymn 521	**Malachi 3:13—4:2a,5–6** Behold, the day comes . . . when all the arrogant and all evildoers will be stubble. But for you . . . the sun of righteousness shall rise.	**Psalm 98:5–10** *or* **Refrain** (Ps. 96:13): The Lord will judge the world with righteousness. *Psalm 98* 5,6/7,8/9,10
Year C Proper 29 Closest to Nov. 23 (Christ the King) Hymn 522 or 106	**Jeremiah 23:1–6** The days are coming . . . I will raise up for David a righteous Branch, and he shall reign as king.	**Psalm 46** *or* **Refrain:** The Lord of hosts is with us; the God of Jacob is our stronghold. *Psalm 46* 1,2,3/5,6,7/9,10,11

SECOND LESSON	ALLELUIA	GOSPEL
2 Thessalonians 1:1–5(6–10)11–12 This is evidence of the righteous judgment of God, that you may be made worthy of the kingdom of God, for which you are suffering.	**Alleluia** *Ad libitum*	**Luke 19:1–10** Zacchaeus stood and said to the Lord, Behold, Lord, the half of my goods I give to the poor; and if I have defrauded any one of anything, I restore it fourfold. And Jesus said to him, Today salvation has come to this house.
2 Thess. 2:13—3:5 The Lord is faithful; he will strengthen you and guard you from evil.	**Alleluia** (Matt. 24:42,44) Be watchful and ready,* for you know not when the Son of Man is coming.	**Luke 20:27(28–33)34–38** There came to him some Sadducees, those who say there is no resurrection. He is not the God of the dead, but of the living; for all live to him.
2 Thess. 3:6–13 Some of you are living in idleness. Such persons we command . . . to do their work.	**Alleluia** (Rev. 2:10) Be faithful until death, says the Lord,* and I will give you the crown of life.	**Luke 21:5–19** The days will come when there shall not be left here one stone upon another. Nation will rise against nation. But not a hair of your head will perish.
Colossians 1:11–20 He is the image of the invisible God, the first-born of all creation . . . all things were created through him and for him.	**Alleluia** (Mark 11:10) Blessed is the kingdom of our father David that is coming;* blessed is he who comes in the name of the Lord.	**Luke 23:35–43** This is the King of the Jews. Jesus, remember me. *or* **Luke 19:29–38** Blessed is the King who comes in the name of the Lord! Peace in heaven and glory in the highest!

Holy Days

HOLY DAYS	FIRST LESSON	PSALM
St. Andrew November 30 Hymn 566	**Deut. 30:11–14** This commandment which I command you this day is not too hard for you. The word is very near you; it is in your mouth and in your heart, so that you can do it.	**Psalm 19:1–6** *or* **Refrain:** Their message has gone out to the ends of the world. *Psalm 19* 1,2/3,4/5,6
St. Thomas December 21 Hymn 99	**Habakkuk 2:1–4** Behold, he whose soul is not upright in him shall fail, but the righteous shall live by faith.	**Psalm 126** *or* **Refrain:** Those who sowed with tears will reap with songs of joy. *Psalm 126* 1,2/3,4/5,7
St. Stephen December 26 Hymn 549	**Jeremiah 26:1–9,12–15** The Lord sent me to prophesy against this house. Know for certain that if you put me to death you will bring innocent blood upon yourselves.	**Psalm 31:1–5** *or* **Refrain:** Into your hands I commend my spirit. *Psalm 31* 1,2/3,4/7,16

SECOND LESSON	ALLELUIA	GOSPEL
Romans 10:8b–18	**Alleluia**	**Matthew 4:18–22**
The word is near you, on your lips and in your heart. But how are men to call upon him in whom they have not believed? And how are they to hear without a preacher?	(Matt. 4:19) Come and follow me, says the Lord,* and I will make you fishers of men.	As Jesus walked by the Sea of Galilee, he saw two brothers . . . Peter and Andrew. Follow me, and I will make you fishers of men.
Hebrews 10:35—11:1	**Alleluia**	**John 20:24–29**
We are not of those who shrink back and are destroyed, but of those who have faith and keep their souls. Now faith is the assurance of things hoped for, the conviction of things not seen.	(John 20:29) You believe in me, Thomas, because you have seen me;* blessed are those who have not seen and yet believe.	Eight days later, his disciples were again in the house, and Thomas was with them. Jesus . . . said to Thomas, Put your finger here, and see my hands. Thomas answered him, My Lord and my God!
Acts 6:8—7:2a,51c–60	**Alleluia**	**Matthew 23:34–39**
Stephen said: Brethren and fathers, hear me. As your fathers did, so do you. And as they were stoning Stephen, he prayed, Lord Jesus, receive my spirit.	(Psalm 118:26,27) Blessed is he who comes in the name of the Lord; God is the Lord; he has shined upon us.	I send you prophets and wise men . . . some of whom you will scourge in your synagogues and persecute. O Jerusalem . . . killing the prophets and stoning those who are sent to you!

St. John	**Exodus 33:18–23**	**Psalm 92:1–4,11–14**
December 27	Moses said, I pray thee, show me thy glory. And he said, I will make all my goodness pass before you, and will proclaim before you my name.	*or* **Refrain:** The righteous shall flourish like a palm tree. *Psalm 92* 1,2/11,12/13,14
Hymn 437		

Holy Innocents	**Jeremiah 31:15–17**	**Psalm 124**
December 28	A voice is heard in Ramah, lamentation and bitter weeping. Rachel is weeping for her children; she refuses to be comforted for her children, because they are not.	*or* **Refrain:** We have escaped like a bird from the snare of the fowler. *Psalm 124* 1,2/3,4/5,6/7,8
Hymn 112 (First tune, hymn 13) or 34		

Confession of St. Peter	**Acts 4:8–13**	**Psalm 23**
January 18	Peter, filled with the Holy Spirit, said . . . Rulers of the people and elders . . . be it known to you all . . . that by the name of Jesus . . . this man is standing before you well.	*or* **Refrain:** The Lord is my shepherd; I shall not be in want. *Psalm 23* 2,3/4ab,4cd/5,6
Hymn 384		

SECOND LESSON	ALLELUIA	GOSPEL
1 John 1:1–9	**Alleluia**	**John 21:19b–24**
This is the message we have heard from him and proclaim to you, that God is light and in him is no darkness at all.	We praise you, O God, we acclaim you as Lord:* the glorious company of apostles praise you.	Peter saw . . . the disciple whom Jesus loved. He said to Jesus, Lord, what about this man? . . . If it is my will that he remain until I come, what is that to you? This is the disciple who is bearing witness to these things.
Revelation 21:1–7	**Alleluia**	**Matthew 2:13–18**
Behold, the dwelling of God is with men. He will dwell with them, and they shall be his people, and God himself will be with them; he will wipe every tear from their eyes, and death shall be no more.	We praise you, O God, we acclaim you as Lord:* the white-robed army of martyrs praise you.	Herod . . . was in a furious rage, and he sent and killed all the male children in Bethlehem and in all that region who were two years old or under, according to the time he had ascertained from the wise men.
1 Peter 5:1–4	**Alleluia**	**Matthew 16:13–19**
Tend the flock of God that is your charge . . . not as domineering over those in your charge but being examples to the flock.	(Matt. 16:18) You are Peter, and on this rock I will build my church;* and the gates of hell shall not prevail against it.	Jesus said to them, But who do you say that I am? Simon Peter replied, You are the Christ, the Son of the living God.

Conversion of St. Paul	**Acts 26:9–21**	**Psalm 67**
January 25	I journeyed to	*or*
Hymn 114	Damascus. I saw on the	**Refrain:** Let the
	way a light . . .	peoples praise you, O
	brighter than the sun. I	God; let all the peoples
	heard a voice saying to	praise you.
	me . . . Saul, Saul,	*Psalm 67*
	why do you persecute	1,2/4/6,7
	me?	
The Presentation of Our Lord Jesus Christ	**Malachi 3:1–4**	**Psalm 84:1–6**
February 2	The Lord whom you	*or*
Hymn 115 or 116	seek will suddenly	**Refrain:** How dear to
	come to his temple. He	me is your dwelling, O
	will purify the sons of	Lord of hosts.
	Levi.	*Psalm 84*
		1,2/3,4/5,6
St. Matthias	**Acts 1:15–26**	**Psalm 15**
February 24	"His office let another	*or*
Hymn 136	take." One of these	**Refrain:** The righteous
	men must become with	shall abide upon God's
	us a witness to his	holy hill.
	resurrection. And they	*Psalm 15*
	cast lots . . . and the	1,2/3,4/5,6/7
	lot fell on Matthias; and	
	he was enrolled with	
	the eleven apostles.	

SECOND LESSON	CHANT BEFORE GOSPEL	GOSPEL
Gal. 1:11–24	**Alleluia**	**Matthew 10:16–22**
The Gospel which was preached by me is not man's gospel, . . . it came through a revelation of Jesus Christ. For you have heard . . . how I persecuted the Church of God.	(John 15:16) I chose you and appointed you that you should go and bear fruit,* and that your fruit should abide.	I send you out as sheep in the midst of wolves; so be wise as serpents and innocent as doves. Beware of men; for they will flog you in their synagogues. He who endures to the end will be saved.
Hebrews 2:14–18	**Alleluia**	**Luke 2:22–40**
Since . . . children share in flesh and blood, he . . . partook of the same nature. He had to be made like his brethren . . . so that he might become a merciful and faithful high priest.	(Luke 2:32) He is the Light to enlighten the nations,* and the glory of your people Israel.	When the time came for their purification according to the law of Moses, they brought him up to Jerusalem to present him to the Lord.
Phil. 3:13–21	**Alleluia**	**John 15:1,6–16**
Let those of us who are mature be thus minded; and if in anything you are otherwise minded, God will reveal that also to you. Only let us hold true to what we have attained.	(John 15:16) I chose you and appointed you that you should go and bear fruit,* and that your fruit should abide. *In Lent* **Tract:** Psalm 112:1–3,6 (*Omit the initial Hallelujah*) *or* **Verse** (*Same as Alleluia verse*)	I am the true vine, and my Father is the vinedresser. If a man does not abide in me, he is cast forth as a branch. You did not choose me, but I chose you.

HOLY DAYS	FIRST LESSON	PSALM
St. Joseph March 19 Hymn 504	**2 Samuel 7:4,8–16** Say . . . to David . . . I will raise up your offspring . . . and I will establish his kingdom. I will be his father, and he shall be my son. I will not take my steadfast love from him.	**Psalm 89:1–4,26–29** *or* **Refrain:** I will establish his line for ever. *Psalm 89* 1,2/3,4/26,27/28,29
The Annunciation April 25 Hymn 118 or 317	**Isaiah 7:10–14** Therefore the Lord himself will give you a sign. Behold, a young woman shall conceive and bear a son.	**Psalm 40:5–10** *or* **Canticle 3 or 15** *or* **Refrain** (Heb. 10:7): Behold, I come to do your will, O God. *Psalm 40* 5,6/7,8/9,11
St. Mark April 25 Hymn 403	**Isaiah 52:7–10** How beautiful upon the mountains are the feet of him who brings good tidings, who publishes peace.	**Psalm 2:7–10** *or* **Refrain:** You are my Son; this day have I begotten you. *Psalm 2* 7,8/9,10/11,13

SECOND LESSON	CHANT BEFORE GOSPEL	GOSPEL
Romans 4:13–18 The promise to Abraham . . . depends on faith, in order that the promise may rest on grace and be guaranteed . . . also to those who share the faith of Abraham, for he is the father of us all.	**Verse** (Ps. 84:3) Happy are they who dwell in your house;* they will always be praising you. or **Tract:** Psalm 112:1–3,6 *(Omit the initial Hallelujah)* *In Easter Season* **Alleluia** *(Same as Verse before the Gospel)*	**Luke 2:41–52** Son, why have you treated us so? Behold, your father and I have been looking for you. Did you not know that I must be in my Father's house? Jesus went down with them and came to Nazareth, and was obedient to them.
Hebrews 10:5–10 When Christ came into the world, he said . . . A body hast thou prepared for me.	**Verse** (John 1:14) The Word was made flesh and dwelt among us,* and we beheld his glory. or **Tract:** Psalm 132:11–15 *In Easter Season* **Alleluia** *(Same as Verse before the Gospel)*	**Luke 1:26–38** In the sixth month the Angel Gabriel was sent . . . to a virgin. You will conceive and bear a son, and you shall call his name Jesus. Let it be to me according to your word.
Eph. 4:7–8,11–16 His gifts were that some should be apostles, some prophets, some evangelists, some pastors and teachers . . . for building up the body of Christ.	**Alleluia** (1 Cor. 1:23,24) We preach a Christ who was crucified;* he is the power and the wisdom of God.	**Mark 1:1–15** The beginning of the gospel of Jesus Christ, the Son of God. In those days Jesus came . . . and was baptised. or **Mark 16:15–20** Go into all the world and preach the gospel to the whole creation.

St. Philip and St. James May 1 Hymn 361	Isaiah 30:18–21 Your eyes shall see your Teacher. And your ears shall hear a word behind you saying, This is the way, walk in it.	Psalm 119:33–40 *or* **Refrain:** Teach me, O Lord, the way of your statutes. *Psalm 119* 34,35/37,38/39,40
The Visitation of the Virgin Mary May 31 Hymn 117	Zeph. 3:14–18a Sing aloud, O daughter of Zion. The Lord your God is in your midst. He will rejoice over you with gladness, he will renew you in his love.	Psalm 113 *or* **Canticle 9** *or* **Refrain:** Let the Name of the Lord be praised, from this time forth for evermore. *Psalm 113* 1,4/5,6/7,8
St. Barnabas June 11 Hymn 517	Isaiah 42:5–12 I have given you as a covenant to the people, a light to the nations, to open the eyes of the blind, to bring out the prisoners from the dungeon, from the prison those who sit in darkness.	Psalm 112 *or* **Refrain:** Happy are they who have given to the poor. *Psalm 112* 1,2/3,4/5,6/7,9
John the Baptist June 24 Hymn 9 or 10	Isaiah 40:1–11 A voice cries, In the wilderness prepare the way of the Lord, make straight in the desert a highway for our God.	Psalm 85:7–13 *or* **Refrain:** Show us your mercy, O Lord, and grant us your salvation. *Psalm 85* 8,9/10,11/12,13

2 Cor. 4:1–6	Alleluia	John 14:6–14
We refuse to practice cunning or to tamper with God's word, but by the open statement of the truth, we would commend ourselves to every man's conscience in the sight of God.	(John 14:6,9) I am the way, the truth, and the life;* whoever has seen me has seen the Father.	Philip said to him, Lord show us the Father. Jesus said . . . Do you not believe that I am in the Father and the Father in me?

Colossians 3:12–17	Alleluia	Luke 1:39–49
Let the word of Christ dwell in you. And whatever you do, in word and deed, do everything in the name of the Lord Jesus.	(Luke 1:45) Blessed is the Virgin Mary, because she believed* that the Lord's promise to her would be fulfilled.	Mary arose and went . . . to a city of Judah . . . and greeted Elizabeth. Elizabeth heard the greeting . . . the babe leaped in her womb. Mary said, My soul magnifies the Lord.

Acts 11:19–30; 13:1–3	Alleluia	Matthew 10:7–16
Now in the church at Antioch there were prophets and teachers, Barnabas . . . and Saul. The Holy Spirit said, Set apart for me Barnabas and Saul for the work to which I have called them.	We praise you, O God, we acclaim you as Lord:* the glorious company of apostles praise you.	The kingdom of heaven is at hand. Heal the sick, raise the dead, cleanse lepers, cast out demons. You received without pay, give without pay.

Acts 13:14b–26	Alleluia	Luke 1:57–80
John had preached a baptism of repentance to all . . . Israel. After me one is coming, the sandals of whose feet I am not worthy to untie.	(Luke 1:76) You shall be called the prophet of the Most High,* for you will go before the Lord to prepare his way.	Elizabeth . . . gave birth to a son. And on the eighth day they came to circumcise the child. His mother said . . . He shall be called John.

St. Peter and St. Paul	**Ezekiel 34:11–16**	**Psalm 87**
June 29 Hymn 437	Thus says the Lord God . . . I myself will search for my sheep. As a shepherd . . . I will bring them out from the peoples . . . I will feed them.	*or* **Refrain:** Glorious things are spoken of you, O city of our God. *Psalm 87* 1,2/3,4/5,6
Independence Day	**Deut. 10:17–21**	**Psalm 145:1–9**
July 4 Hymn 144	Your God is God of gods . . . who is not partial and takes no bribe. He executes justice for the fatherless and the widow, and loves the sojourner, giving him food and clothing.	*or* **Refrain:** I will exalt you, O God my King, and bless your Name for ever and ever. *Psalm 145* 2,3/4,5/6,7/8,9
or **Votive For the** **Nation**	**Isaiah 26:1–8** Open the gates, that the righteous nation which keeps faith may enter in. Thou dost keep him in perfect peace, whose mind is stayed on thee.	**Psalm 47** *or* **Refrain:** Proclaim the glory of the Lord among the nations. *Psalm 47* 1,2/7,8/9,10

SECOND LESSON	ALLELUIA	GOSPEL
2 Timothy 4:1–8	**Alleluia**	**John 21:15–19**
The time of my departure has come. I have fought the good fight, I have finished the race, I have kept the faith.	(Rev. 2:10) Be faithful until death, says the Lord,* and I will give you the crown of life.	Jesus said to Simon Peter, Simon . . . do you love me? Feed my lambs . . . Tend my sheep . . . Feed my sheep.
Hebrews 11:8–16	**Alleluia**	**Matthew 5:43–48**
They desire a better country, that is, a heavenly one. Therefore God is not ashamed to be called their God, for he has prepared for them a city.	(Psalm 108:3) I will confess you among the peoples, O Lord;* I will sing praises to you among the nations.	I say to you, Love your enemies and pray for those who persecute you, so that you may be sons of your Father who is in heaven. . . . You, therefore, must be perfect, as your heavenly Father is perfect.
Romans 13:1–10	**Alleluia**	**Mark 12:13–17**
Pay all of them their due, taxes to whom taxes are due . . . respect to whom respect is due, honor to whom honor is due. Owe no one anything, except to love one another; for he who loves his neighbor has fulfilled the law.	*As above*	Render to Caesar the things that are Caesar's, and to God the things that are God's.

St. Mary Magdalene July 22 Hymn 69	**Judith 9:1,11–14** Judith cried out to the Lord . . . Thy power depends not upon numbers, nor thy might upon men of strength; for thou art God of the lowly. Cause thy whole nation . . . to know . . . that thou art God.	**Psalm 42:1–7** *or* **Refrain:** As the deer longs for the water-brooks, so longs my soul for you, O God. *Psalm 42* 2,3/4,5/6,7
St. James July 25 Hymn 132	**Jeremiah 45:1–5** Thus says the Lord; Behold, what I have built I am breaking down. Do you seek great things for yourself? Seek them not.	**Psalm 7:1–10** *or* **Refrain:** God is my shield and defense; he is the savior of the true in heart. *Psalm 7* 1,2/7,8/9,10
The Transfiguration of Our Lord August 6 Hymn 119 or 571 Entrance Hymn 587	**Exodus 34:29–35** When Moses came down from Mount Sinai . . . Moses did not know that the skin of his face shone because he had been talking with God.	**Psalm 99:5–9** *or* **Refrain:** Proclaim the greatness of the Lord our God; he is the Holy One. *Psalm 99* 1,2/6,7/8,9

SECOND LESSON	ALLELUIA	GOSPEL
2 Cor. 5:14–18	**Alleluia**	**John 20:11–18**
If anyone is in Christ, he is a new creation; the old has passed away, behold, the new has come. All this is from God, who through Christ reconciled us to himself and gave us the ministry of reconciliation.	(Hymn 97:4,5) Tell us, Mary, what did you see on the way?* I saw the glory of the risen Christ; I saw his empty tomb.	Mary stood weeping outside the tomb. Jesus said to her, Do not hold me . . . but go to my brethren and say to them, I am ascending to my father. Mary Magdalene went and said to the disciples, I have seen the Lord.
Acts 11:27—12:3	**Alleluia**	**Matthew 20:20–28**
Herod the king laid violent hands upon some who belonged to the church. He killed James the brother of John with the sword.	(John 15:16) I chose you and appointed you that you should go and bear fruit,* and that your fruit should abide.	The mother of the sons of Zebedee came up to him with her sons, and . . . asked him . . . Command that these two sons of mine may sit, one at your right hand and one at your left.
2 Peter 1:13–21	**Alleluia**	**Luke 9:28–36**
We were eyewitnesses to his glory. This is my beloved Son. We heard this from heaven, for we were with him on the holy mountain.	(Matt. 17:5) This is my Son, my Beloved,* with whom I am well pleased.	He took with him Peter and James and John, and went up on the mountain to pray. The appearance of his countenance was altered. And behold, two men talked with him, Moses and Elijah. This is my Son.

	FIRST LESSON	PSALM
St. Mary the Virgin August 15 Hymn 117	Isaiah 61:10–11 I will greatly rejoice in the Lord, my soul shall exalt in my God. The Lord will cause righteousness and praise to spring forth before all the nations.	Psalm 34:1–9 *or* **Refrain:** Proclaim with me the greatness of the Lord our God. *Psalm 34* 1,2/3,5/7,8/9,10
St. Bartholomew August 24 Hymn 135	Deut. 18:15–18 The Lord said . . . I will raise up for them a prophet like you from among their brethren; and I will put my words in his mouth, and he shall speak to them all that I command him.	Psalm 91:1–4 *or* **Refrain:** He shall give his angels charge over you. *Psalm 91* 1/2/3/4
Holy Cross Day September 14 Hymn 336 or 357	Isaiah 45:21–25 Turn to me and be saved, all the ends of the earth! For I am God, and there is no other.	Psalm 91:1–4 *or* **Refrain:** All the ends of the earth have seen the victory of our God. *Psalm 98* 1,2/3,4/8,10

SECOND LESSON	ALLELUIA	GOSPEL
Galatians 4:4–7	**Alleluia**	**Luke 1:46–55**
When the time had fully come, God sent forth his Son, born of woman, born under the law, to redeem those who were under the law, so that we might receive adoption as sons.	(Luke 1:46) My soul proclaims the greatness of the Lord,* my spirit rejoices in God my Savior.	Mary said, My soul magnifies the Lord, and my spirit rejoices in God my Savior, for he has regarded the low estate of his handmaiden.
1 Cor. 4:9–15	**Alleluia**	**Luke 22:24–30**
I think that God has exhibited us apostles as last of all, like men sentenced to death. We are fools for Christ's sake.	We praise you, O God, we acclaim you as Lord:* the glorious company of apostles praise you.	A dispute also arose among them, which of them was to be regarded as the greatest. Let the greatest among you become as the youngest, and the leader as one who serves.
Phil. 2:5–11	**Alleluia**	**John 12:31–36a**
Being found in human form he humbled himself and became obedient unto death, even death on a cross.	We adore you, O Christ, and we bless you,* because by your holy cross you have redeemed the world.	Now is the judgment of this world, now shall the ruler of this world be cast out; and I, when I am lifted up from the earth, will draw all men to myself.
or **Gal. 6:14–18** Far be it from me to glory except in the cross of our Lord Jesus Christ.		

St. Matthew September 21 Hymn 134	**Proverbs 3:1–6** My son, do not forget my teaching. Trust in the Lord with all your heart, and do not rely on your own insight. In all your ways acknowledge him, and he will make straight your paths.	**Psalm 119:33–40** *or* **Refrain:** Teach me, O Lord, the way of your statutes. *Psalm 119* 34,35/37,38/39,40
St. Michael and All Angels September 29 Hymn 121 or 123	**Genesis 28:10–17** Jacob came to a certain place. And he dreamed that there was a ladder set up on the earth, and the top of it reached to heaven; and behold, the angels of God were ascending and descending on it.	**Psalm 103:19–22** *or* **Refrain:** Bless the Lord, O my soul. *Psalm 103* 19/20/21/22
St. Luke October 18 Hymn 515 or 516	**Ecclesiastes 38:1–4,6–10,12–14** Honor the physician with the honor due him, according to your need of him, for the Lord created him; for healing comes from the most high.	**Psalm 147:1–7** *or* **Refrain:** The Lord heals the brokenhearted and binds up their wounds. *Psalm 147* 1,2/4,5/6,7
St. James of Jerusalem October 23 Hymn 129	**Acts 15:12–22a** James replied . . . My judgment is that we should not trouble those of the Gentiles who turn to God, but should write to them to abstain from the pollutions of idols and from unchastity.	**Psalm 1** *or* **Refrain:** Happy are they whose delight is in the law of the Lord. *Psalm 1* 1,2/3,4/5,6

SECOND LESSON	ALLELUIA	GOSPEL
2 Tim. 3:14–17 All scripture is inspired by God and profitable for teaching, for reproof, for correction, and for training in righteousness.	**Alleluia** We praise you, O God, we acclaim you as Lord:* the glorious company of apostles praise you.	**Matthew 9:9–13** As Jesus passed on from there, he saw a man called Matthew sitting at the tax office; and he said to him, Follow me. He rose and followed him.
Revelation 12:7–12 Now war arose in heaven, Michael and his angels fighting against the dragon; and the dragon and his angels fought, but they were defeated and there was no longer any place for them in heaven.	**Alleluia** (Ps. 148:1,2) Praise the Lord from the heavens;* praise him all you angels.	**John 1:47–51** Jesus said to Nathanael, Truly, truly, I say to you, you will see heaven opened, and the angels of God ascending and descending upon the Son of man.
2 Timothy 4:5–13 I have fought the good fight, I have finished the race, I have kept the faith. Do your best to come to me soon. Luke alone is with me.	**Alleluia** (John 15:16) I chose you and appointed you that you should go and bear fruit,* and that your fruit should abide.	**Luke 4:14–21** Jesus came to Nazareth. There was given to him the book of the prophet Isaiah. The Spirit of the Lord is upon me. Today this scripture has been fulfilled in your hearing.
1 Cor. 15:1–11 I delivered to you as of first importance what I also received, that Christ died for our sins . . . that he was raised on the third day . . . then he appeared to James, then to all the apostles.	**Alleluia** We praise you, O God, we acclaim you as Lord;* the white-robed army of martyrs praise you.	**Matthew 13:54–58** Where did this man get this wisdom and these mighty works? Is not this the carpenter's son? Is not his mother called Mary? And are not his brothers James and Joseph?

St. Simon and St. Jude October 28 Hymn 124	**Deut. 32:1–4** Give ear, O heavens, and I will speak. May my teaching drop as the rain. I will proclaim the name of the Lord.	**Psalm 119:89–96** *or* **Refrain:** O Lord, your word is everlasting. *Psalm 119* 90,91/92,93/94,96
All Saints Day November 1 Hymn 130 or 129 Entrance Hymn 599	**Ecclus. 44:1–10,13–14** There are some . . . who have left a name . . . some who have no memorial. Their glory will not be blotted out.	**Psalm 149** *or* **Refrain:** Sing to the Lord a new song. *Psalm 149* 2,3/4,5/6,7/8,9
or this	**Ecclus. 2:(1–6)7–11** You who fear the Lord, wait for his mercy. Consider the ancient generations and see: who ever trusted in the Lord and was put to shame?	**Psalm 149** *As above*
Thanksgiving Day Hymn 137	**Deuteronomy 8:1–3,6–10(17–20)** You shall keep the commandments of the Lord your God. And you shall eat and be full, and you shall bless the Lord your God for the good land he has given you.	**Psalm 65:9–14** *or* **Refrain:** You crown the year with your goodness, O Lord. *Psalm 65* 9,10/11,12/13,14

SECOND LESSON	ALLELUIA	GOSPEL
Eph. 2:13–22	**Alleluia**	**John 15:17–27**
You are no longer strangers and sojourners, but you are fellow citizens with the saints and members of the household of God.	We praise you, O God, we acclaim you as Lord;* the glorious company of apostles praise you.	This I command you, to love one another. If the world hates you, know that it has hated me before it hated you. I chose you out of the world, therefore the world hates you.
Rev. 7:2–4,9–17	**Alleluia**	**Matthew 5:1–12**
Who are these, clothed in white robes? These are they who have come out of the great tribulation.	(Matt. 11:28) Come to me, all who labor and are heavy laden,* and I will give you rest.	Blessed are the poor in spirit, for theirs is the kingdom of heaven.
Eph. 1:(11–14)15–23	**Alleluia**	**Luke 6:20–26(27–36)**
Because I have heard of your faith in the Lord Jesus and your love toward all the saints, I do not cease to give thanks for you.	As *above*	Blessed are you poor, for yours is the kingdom of God.
James 1:17–18,21–27	**Alleluia**	**Matthew 6:25–33**
Every good endowment and every perfect gift is from above, coming down from the Father of lights with whom there is no variation or shadow due to change.	(Ps. 118:1) Give thanks to the Lord, for he is good;* his mercy endures for ever.	Do not be anxious about your life, what you shall eat or what you shall drink, nor about your body, what you shall put on. Seek first his kingdom and his righteousness, and all these things shall be yours as well.

Hymn List

2	O Come, O come, Emmanuel!	9	Hark! a thrilling
10	On Jordan's bank	3	Wake, awake
6	Creator of the stars	11	The King shall come
329	How bright appears	440	Watchman, tell us
36	What child is this	27	Hark! the herald
13	While Shepherds watched	42	Angels we have heard
17	I know a rose-tree	117	Sing of Mary
35	He whom joyous	21	O Little town
48	Earth has many	30	The first Nowell
53	Songs of thankfulness	52	As with gladness
329	How bright appears	492	From glory to glory
253	Spread, O spread	302	O that I had
298	The Great Creator	539	Soon may the last
56	Kind Maker of the world	59	Lord, who throughout
344	O love, how deep	522	Lord Christ, when
61	The glory of these	289	O God, our help
501	O Lord, and Master	335	Glory be to Jesus
89	At the Lamb's high feast	91	The strife is o'er
99	O sons and daughters	94	Come, ye faithful
90	He is risen	347	Alleluia, sing to Jesus
98	That Easter Day	352	Crown him with many
376	Come down, O love divine	111	Spirit of mercy
108	O come, Creator Spirit		
195	Father, we thank thee	258	Christ is the world's
462	Jesus, the very thought	326	To the Name
276	Now thank we all our God	314	We sing of God
255	Awake, thou spirit	485	Jesus, thou joy
388	I love thy kingdom	479	Love divine
385	Glorious things of thee	289	O God, our help

[203]

AUGUST–SEPTEMBER	384	Christ is made
	278	All people that
	380	Put forth, O God
	300	Before the Lord
	282	Praise my soul
	149	Awake, my soul (M)
	162	O God, creation's (E)
OCTOBER–NOVEMBER	285	The God of Abraham
	577	Awake, my soul, stretch
	361	Thou art the Way
	370	Spirit divine
	484	Lift up your heads
	158	O splendor of God's (M)
	181	The duteous day (E)

M and E denote entrance hymns appropriate to Morning and Evening celebrations respectively

124711

356	At the Name of Jesus		314	We sing of God
345	The King of love		263	In Christ there is
307	Most High, omnipotent		287	Give praise and glory
347	Alleluia, sing to Jesus		489	Lord, dismiss us
343	Praise to the holiest		542	Jesus shall reign
284	My God, how wonderful		273	Holy God, we praise
228	Only-begotten, Word of God		600	Ye holy angels bright
585	Jerusalem, my happy home		424	Jesus, lead the way
442	O very God of very God		477	God himself is with us
418	Blest are the pure		511	Jesus, thou divine
376	Come down, O love divine		569	Lo! what a cloud
298	The great Creator		260	How wondrous and great

Alleluia Verses

For use *ad libitum* when appointed in the Proper. Any of the verses appointed for particular days or seasons may also be used, provided that it is congruent with the Gospel Reading which follows.

1. Show me your ways, O Lord;*
   lead me in your truth and teach me. *(Psalm 25:3,4)*

2. I will bless the Lord at all times;*
   his praise shall ever be in my mouth. *(Psalm 34:1)*

3. Your love, O Lord, for ever will I sing;*
   from age to age my mouth will proclaim your
   faithfulness. *(Psalm 89:1)*

4. Sing to the Lord and bless his Name;*
   proclaim the good news of his salvation from
   day to day. *(Psalm 96:2)*

5. The commandments of the Lord are sure;*
   they stand fast for ever and ever. *(Psalm 111:7,8)*

6. Open my eyes, O Lord,*
   that I may see the wonders of your law. *(Psalm 119:18)*

7. Give me understanding, O Lord,*
   and I shall keep your law with all my heart. *(Psalm 119:34)*

8. Your word is a lantern to my feet*
   and a light upon my path. *(Psalm 119:105)*

9. The Lord is faithful in all his words*
   and merciful in all his deeds. *(Psalm 145:14)*

10. How good it is to sing praises to our God;*
    how pleasant it is to honor him with praise. *(Psalm 147:1)*

11. Worship the Lord, O Jerusalem;*
    praise your God, O Zion. *(Psalm 147:13)*

12. Man shall not live by bread alone,*
    but by every word that proceeds from the
    mouth of God. *(Matt. 4:4)*

13. Your words, O Lord, are spirit and life;*
    you have the words of everlasting life. *(John 6:63,68)*

14. The word of the Lord stands fast for ever;*
    his word is the Gospel preached to you. *(1 Peter 1:25)*

DATE DUE

HIGHSMITH 45-102   PRINTED IN U.S.A.